the
Longing

Embracing the Deepest Truth
of Who You Are

JOEY O'CONNOR

Revell
Grand Rapids, Michigan

© 2004 by Joey O'Connor

Published by Fleming H. Revell
a division of Baker Publishing Group
P.O. Box 6287, Grand Rapids, MI 49516-6287
www.revellbooks.com

Printed in the United States of America

Library of Congress Cataloging-in-Publication Data
O'Connor, Joey, 1964–
        The longing : embracing the deepest truth of who you are / Joey O'Connor.
            p.   cm.
        Includes bibliographical references.
        ISBN 0-8007-1848-8 (casebound)
        1. Christian life. I. Title.
    VB4501.3.032 2004
    248.4—dc22   17tlg   2004008065

Unless otherwise indicated, Scripture is taken from the HOLY BIBLE, NEW INTER-NATIONAL VERSION®. NIV®. Copyright © 1973, 1978, 1984 by International Bible Society. Used by permission of Zondervan. All rights reserved.

Scripture marked AMP is taken from the Amplified® Bible, Copyright © 1954, 1958, 1962, 1964, 1965, 1987 by The Lockman Foundation. Used by permission.

Scripture marked Message is taken from *The Message* by Eugene H. Peterson, copyright © 1993, 1994, 1995, 2000, 2001, 2002. Used by permission of NavPress Publishing Group. All rights reserved.

Scripture marked NASB is taken from the New American Standard Bible®, Copyright © 1960, 1962, 1963, 1968, 1971, 1972, 1973, 1975, 1977, 1995 by The Lockman Foundation. Used by permission.

This book is warmly dedicated to

Tom Thompson

*We wanted to confess our sins
but there were no takers.*

Milosz

Contents

ONE

The Fruit of Unanswered Questions

L
ast year, my wife, Krista, and I sat in LAX waiting to board a plane for a much-needed vacation to Hawaii. I was physically present but emotionally stranded. I felt isolated and alone on an imaginary island of "what if" scenarios surrounded by the shark-infested waters of my circling fears. Mentally, I was still sixty miles to the south, back at home, grinding over all the recent changes in my life. Though I was looking forward to our vacation—sleeping in, taking longs walks with Krista, checking out new surf spots on Kauai—I was anything but anchored in the present. At the rate I was going, I'd need six months to unwind.

I flipped open my cell phone and called a close friend, a mentor who had helped me navigate the emotional storms and challenges I'd been through in the past few years. My head was in a literal fog from all the pressure I felt inside. (When I'm feeling overwhelmed, I call it "foggy head.") And the previous two months had been marked by emotional exhaustion and increasing levels of anxiety as my heart reacted to change going on in both my inner and outer worlds. I had just completed a new book and was emotionally spent. The book's completion took six weeks longer than anticipated. And then edits. And more edits. On top of that, the church where I served was going through layoffs and its third reorganization in three years. I saw good friends lose their jobs. I was also initiating the start of a new nonprofit organization designed to minister to the spiritual development and creative vision of artists in the church. My fear of failure was screaming at me like a wild monkey in the trees (the only inhabitants of my island except me).

Nobody was putting pressure on me but me. The convergence of exhaustion, grief, change, and new risks made me feel as if my heart was being lobbed into a tree chipper. It was everything I could do to duck from the ear-splitting screams of my fears and all the monkey crap they were hurling my way. Exhausted, I was on the verge of messing up a really good Hawaiian vacation. I was headed to the islands, an oasis of palm trees and white sandy beaches, but that's not what my heart needed most. I was longing for peace. Longing for rest. Longing for a sense of wholeness that, at this moment, seemed completely out of reach for how disintegrated I felt.

Milan, my friend, and I talked. He encouraged me to let go of "the need to know."

So much of my anxiety was tied to my need to know how everything was going to turn out. Would I still have a job at church when I returned at the end of the summer? With all the departmental changes going on, would I have the same position? Should I jump ship and throw myself full-time into this new nonprofit? What if the nonprofit failed and I was out of both jobs? What if? What if? What if?

The sharks were circling and the monkeys reaching for another handful.

All I had to do was let go, but letting go meant grasping the invisible, intangible concepts of faith, trust, and hope. Easier said than done.

Whose Are You?

"Anxiety is the mark of spiritual insecurity," wrote Thomas Merton, the late Trappist monk and spiritual writer. "It is the fruit of unanswered questions."[1]

My anxiety was the fruit of unanswered questions about my future and the refusal to trust in the goodness of God, who has proven his faithfulness and unconditional love throughout my life. Practical considerations aside, I was asking an entirely wrong set of questions. Much like the fear-filled Peter looking at the wind and crashing waves after Jesus asked him to step out of the boat, I had taken my eyes off what was really true about my life. I wanted answers to the unknown future instead of trusting that the most important questions had already been answered. Like Peter, I was sinking deeper and deeper into the abyss of my worries and uncertainties.

> Anxiety is the mark of spiritual insecurity. It is the fruit of unanswered questions.

I was looking at Joey instead of Jesus. I was staring at the invisible wind of my imaginary fears, all of them illusions masking the truth of what was real in my life.

If you were to do a preflight checklist of my life, you'd probably ask, "What in the heck are you so worried about?" The most important questions—Does God love me? Does God accept me? Does my life have a clear purpose? Do I have a meaningful relationship with my wife and kids? Do I have deep, lasting friendships?—had already been answered. All I needed to do now was live from the center of these truths. Sounds good on paper, but for me, this is really hard to do at times.

Our hearts bear the marks of brokenness that reflect the brokenness Christ bore on the cross on our behalf. The truth of our existence is that we are more broken than bulletproof. Our hearts and lives are not always what they appear. We are far more content with the shallow facades of appearances than with a vibrant life pocked with the scars of authentic human struggle.

And beneath the brokenness, there is something deeper inside of us. Something truer about ourselves than we ever imagined. Deep inside the very core of our heart is a longing. An incessant longing that won't go away. It's a longing that demands an answer. Left unanswered, the longing accesses what is readily available in our heart, in most cases our brokenness, to get our attention. In my case, the longing buried itself deep inside my heart and tried to speak to me through my anxiety. My anxiety, the very thing I thought was destroying me, was this masked longing trying to get my attention in order to free me. But the road to freedom can be a very circuitous route. It often takes many laps around the same issue or problem before we begin to formulate the real question our heart is asking.

So, if anxiety is the fruit of unanswered questions, what then are the questions? When did the questions first go unanswered? Long ago, when and where were the seeds of unanswered questions first planted that are just now bearing the fruit of anxiety, doubt, and fear? For many of us, the alienation and anxiety we experience in our lives and relationships begin far before we even know how to articulate the questions. Long before we even know we have a longing. A baby left alone a minute or so too long experiences the terrifying reality of being left alone—what do they call it?—*separation anxiety*? We are made for relationship, and the absence of a loving presence, a little too much and a little too long, can stamp the indelible stain of separation on our hearts for the rest of our lives. In other cases, screaming voices and fighting parents leave young children ducking for cover. A teenager's parents get divorced and the teenager blames himself. As children, we felt conflict. Even if we lived in the best of homes, we sensed times of tension. And the questions began to form. Do I belong? Do I have a place and a voice here? Am I loved for just being me or is there another standard? Just what are the unwritten rules? Who is safe? Who can I trust?

Then we go to school. That's where the real tension begins to build. School is a place where we are encouraged to ask questions about the three Rs, but our hearts are silently asking much more important questions. Questions that will ultimately influence who we become as adults. Do I belong? Am I loved unconditionally? Will people like me? Will people accept me for who I am? Will I be chosen? Will I make the team? School is where our hearts learn very quickly that the world is not safe. School is not all bad, of course, because it is a place of forming friendships, a place of learning and discovery. But we also learn how to form alliances, build defenses, and hunker down to avoid the shelling of taunting and teasing. Every playground has its own rules of warfare, and each is like a microcosm of warring nations.

I'm convinced that the longing in our hearts goes back to the places where we spent time as kids. Think of a classroom, a park, a playground, an athletic field, a college classroom, or the home where you grew up. Then name a time or event in connection with this place when you felt chosen or left out, when you felt loved or hated, when you felt accepted or rejected. It will take all of 1.3 seconds for that experience to flip on the radar screen of your heart. Can you see it?

Let that image stay there for a moment or two. You can name names. Describe the setting. Stay in that place long enough, and your heart will go to the movies of your memory as if it happened just a moment or two ago. You can begin to feel feelings and thoughts and emotions that you thought had long since disappeared. This is the place where the real questions of our lives were formed. This is where and when we discovered if we were chosen, loved, and accepted, or not chosen, unloved, and rejected.

One night in the grief recovery class I lead, a woman named Jennifer shared one of her earliest memories of rejection and humiliation. As a young girl, Jennifer was shy and afraid of speaking in front of others. When she was in the third grade, her teacher asked her to stand in front of class and read out loud. Standard stuff for elementary classes, but what Jennifer experienced left an ugly brand on her heart that remains to this day.

Nervous, Jennifer began to read from a book while all the other students looked on. She came upon the word *island* and pronounced it just as it looks, "is-land" instead of saying the word with a silent *s*. When the class heard her mistake, they roared with laughter. Jennifer stood silent as waves of shame and rejection hit her one after the other. The teacher did nothing. Jennifer went back to her seat alone and humiliated, the seed of rejection firmly planted in her heart.

Ever since we were children, our hearts have longed to belong. *This is the longing.* Whether it was our first day of kindergarten, our first tryout, or a move into a new neighborhood, our hearts wanted to feel welcomed. To be one of the gang. We have all longed to *be longed for.* Our hearts have always wanted to be wanted by others, but what all of us have experienced, in different ways, is rejection, like Jennifer.

Many of us can honestly look at our lives and say we've experienced both realities. We made the swim team, but we didn't make the volleyball team. Our parents loved us, but we got our rear kicked at the bike rack. We were accepted to college but rejected by the sorority or fraternity we wanted. We've been chosen and not chosen. Loved and unloved. Accepted and rejected. Nobody gets through childhood unscathed. I believe with all my heart that all of our worry and hand-wringing, strivings and failings, our sins, our addictions, our consummate need for approval and affirmation, our ridiculous talk about living a "balanced life" (which is code for saying that what we really want is control), all of our grasping for more, the compulsive, seemingly elusive search for happiness in a chaotic world, is rooted not in our longing for who we are but *whose* we are.

In the search for identity, we ask, "Who am I?" But we are asking the wrong question. The essence of spiritual identity is knowing in our heart of hearts *whose* we are. If we don't know this, our lives are filled with the fruit of unanswered questions. We can't know who we are apart from relationship, and we are made to mirror the one who created us, because we were made in the image of God. Our hearts have always longed to hear that we are chosen, loved, and accepted, but what our hearts have heard is the noise of many voices. Cruel voices. Lying voices. Manipulative voices. Controlling voices. The voice of silence. The voice of pain. These voices are like obnoxious, uninvited neighbors who storm into our hearts without knocking and

> The essence of spiritual identity is knowing in our heart of hearts whose we are.

plop down in our living room, expecting us to serve them a cold one and whatever's left in the fridge. Not wanting to offend but hoping they will soon leave, we let the voices chatter on and on. We listen and nod, trying politely to interject our opinion, but the voices dominate and control, dismissing whatever we say, always trying to keep the upper hand in the conversation. This goes on for years. What we don't recognize is that in listening to so many other voices, we've somehow lost our own voice. Some of us don't even know we have one, let alone experience the deeper, quieter Voice calling out to us.

Waking Up to Noise

C. S. Lewis wrote that all the noise and chatter in our life begins the moment our eyes blink open in the shrinking shadows of the early morning light.

> The real problem of the Christian life comes from where people do not look for it. It comes the very moment you wake up each morning. All your wishes and hopes for the day rush at you like wild animals. And the first job each morning consists simply in shoving them all back; listening to that other Voice, taking in that other point of view, letting that other larger, stronger, quieter life come flowing in. And so on, all day. Standing back from all your natural fussings and frettings; coming in out of the wind. We can only do it for moments at first. But from those moments the new sort of life will be spreading through our system; because now we are letting Him work at the right part of us. It is the difference between paint, which is merely laid on the surface, and a dye or stain which soaks right through.[2]

Upon waking, our thoughts rush at us likes wolves eager to devour our to-do list for the day. Our propensity is not to consider who we are or whose we are but what we have to achieve. We wake up to the noise in our minds to do, succeed, conquer, and win. As we scrub and scour in the shower, we are arranging our mental checklists, ordering our day with all of its responsibilities, meetings, appointments, and deadlines. Mentally, we are working hard to accomplish much before any real work gets done. Before we know it, we're stressed from being stressed.

If your home resembles my home in any way, you are mentally multitasking *and* rallying the troops to get ready for school. You know the drill: clothes on, beds made, teeth brushed, hair combed, lunches in backpacks, sugar-laden breakfast consumed, go-go-go!—as we push our back-pack-laden children into the car pool like soldiers ready to parachute into the fields of Normandy.

As we stand in the driveway waving as the kids go off to school, we exhale a sigh of relief. Suddenly, we hear a cry coming from inside our home. It's that obnoxious neighbor again. We dash into the living room, and what do we discover? Curled up underneath a blanket and lying on our couch, that voice picks up right where he left off, barking orders and commands, wondering what in the world it takes to get scrambled eggs, bacon, and a hot cup of coffee around this joint.

Wait. Stop.

Before you get out of bed, there is nothing more important for you to do than stop, lie there quietly for a couple minutes, and listen for that other Voice. Before you say anything, do anything, solve any problem, or even try to formulate what some of the unanswered questions may be in your life—listen for that one true Voice who has been calling you all your life. This is the Voice your heart longs to hear and the words your heart longs to absorb. Words spoken to you by God from the very beginning of time. This Voice comes through words of

Scripture that are as real and alive today as the day they were spoken to Jesus at his baptism.

Out of every word written in this whole book, there is one sentence and one sentence only that I want to start and end with. It contains the words given by a father to his son, right before the start of an incredible three-year journey. They are words that every son, every daughter, every person on this earth has been created to hear. In Matthew 3:17, we read the words that anchored Jesus in the love of his Father. And they are the very words that will answer all the unanswered questions in our lives. They will anchor our lives in the most secure relationship we've ever experienced.

"And a voice from heaven said, 'This is my Son, whom I love; with him I am well pleased'" (NIV).

"And behold, a voice out from heaven said, This is My Son, My Beloved, in Whom I delight!" (AMP).

Read those words again. Let the longing in your heart linger over them. Drop your guard and allow your heart to be immersed in the truth of God's love for you. The longing of God's heart is to connect with the longing in your heart. This longing, his and yours, if you allow it, will penetrate the innermost part of who you are. Hear the Father's voice say to you "You are my son. You are my daughter, whom I love. With you—yes, you—I am well pleased. You give me great pleasure."

Stay with the truth of these words long enough and they will fire hose your sandcastle defenses. The words of this one sentence contain the implicit truth: You are chosen.

You are loved. You are accepted. This is the truth of who you are, and this truth will transform your life. These are the very words your heart has been longing to hear.

You are my beloved. My delight. My chosen, loved, and accepted child.

This is the silent cry of every human heart.

Let the truth of his love for you soak right through you.

When was the last time someone cupped their hands around your face, looked intently in your eyes, and with tenderness said in a soft whisper meant for you alone, "You are my chosen one, whom I love, in whom I'm well pleased." When has someone said to you, "You are my beloved and my delight"? Almost embarrassing, isn't it?

Until we acknowledge this deep, universal need to be chosen, loved, and accepted, we will set out on a directionless expedition in search of the acceptance and belonging that is already ours through the love of God found in Christ Jesus. The whole course of our life is a search for being chosen, loved, and accepted. This is what my heart longed for in the airport, when all I could hear were the exhausting screams of my fears and the uncertainty of my future. It's what your heart longs to hear as you read this book right now.

The Deepest Truth of Who You Are

This book is about developing a vision of the new you. It is about being honest with yourself and admitting that the core longing in your heart is spiritual. It is about realizing the deepest truth of who you are and living out of the truth of God's love for you. In Christ, you are being carefully shaped and carved by the hand of God. When God looks at you, he sees a child who is a completely new creation in Christ. Living as a follower of Christ is the personal, daily integration of the deepest truth of who you are. Despite what you've been told or have experienced, you are not the sum total of your gifts and talents, your strengths and weaknesses, your victories and defeats. You are not your job. You are not your status, your inflated fantasies of greatness or lowest levels of self-hatred. You are not your roles as husband or wife, father or mother, son or daughter, boss or employee, sinner or saint. You are not your net worth in homes, assets, or possessions. Your net worth is in the invisible, inestimable, immeasurable love of God. You are, as St. John of the Cross declared long ago, the beloved of God. To truly live as one who is chosen is a daily journey of choosing to find your identity in Christ and Christ alone.

In Christ, you are a child of God, and all the unanswered questions of life, your deepest longings, are answered in him. So be ready. Once you discover the power of authentically living as a chosen child of God, life as you know it today will forever change. When you discover you are wholly, wonderfully, and unconditionally loved, you will begin to live in that unique, spacious place—that wonderful mystery in which nothing else matters and everything matters. Living with your deepest longing fulfilled in Christ, you will discover the presence of God in your heart to disengage from needing the approval and fickle opinions of your husband or wife. Your mother or father. Friend. Neighbor. Or boss. And while disengaging from the keyhole perspective of others' limited viewpoints and expectations, you will walk in freedom to love them and engage them with the gift of chosenness you have received from God. You will discover the peace that comes with living your own life as God intended and not with a warped caricature of someone else's.

In the following pages we are going to explore both how to live in the fullness of this truth and what keeps us from resting in the transforming love of our Father. Our life experiences have applied many layers of protective coating over our hearts, and stripping away our defenses to allow God inside the deepest parts of who we are is difficult work. Choosing to live as a chosen, loved, and accepted child of God means that you are choosing to live in tension. You are a chosen child of God *and* you live in an imperfect, competitive world that prefers slavery over freedom. You are a beloved child of God *and* some of the most perplexing questions closest to your heart may never be answered. You are an accepted child of God *and* you will still battle rejection, frustration, temptation, sin, and conflict.

And so, as you turn the pages ahead to see who you are as a child of God, let your first steps begin with a prayer of faith. Pray in humble confidence that God's voice will speak to you, and that in hearing his voice, you will find your own voice as a chosen child.

> My father, I abandon myself to you, do unto me whatever you wish. For anything that may please you to do with me, I give you thanks, I am ready for everything, I accept everything. Provided that your holy will be done unto me and all your creatures, I do not wish anything else, my God. I place my soul into your hands, I give it to you, my God, with all the love of my heart, because I feel this need to give myself out of love, to surrender myself totally into your hands, with an infinite confidence, because you are my Father.[3]

Charles de Foucauld

TWO

Named by the Father

The Gospels give us only two public glimpses of God the Father speaking directly to Jesus in the three years that Jesus walked among the small towns and dusty villages of Israel, preaching the good news of his Father's kingdom. For all we read of Jesus speaking about his heavenly Father, we don't read much about father-son talks. Wouldn't you think that for all the amazing work Jesus did on behalf of his Father, he'd receive a few more attaboys from above? At least a little more praise and affirmation? I hoot and holler when my kids stand up on a surfboard at Doheny beach. But when Jesus walks on water, God says absolutely nothing.

Jesus? He can't stop talking about his dad. In the Gospels of Matthew, Mark, Luke, but particularly in John, we see Jesus constantly talking about his father. But it's not the father we'd expect. Joseph, Jesus' earthly father, saved him when he was a baby by whisking him away to Egypt when Herod had it out for Jewish toddlers. For this, Joseph gets only a few pages of press. At twelve years old, when Jesus goes with Joseph and Mary to the temple in Jerusalem, he loses his parents for three whole days to spend time with his true Father. After his parents' exhausting search, Jesus responds to his worried mother, "Didn't you know I had to be in my Father's house?" (Luke 2:49). I wonder if Joseph and Mary threatened to pummel the preteen Jesus into next week?

After his baptism and throughout his three-year ministry, Jesus is always bragging on his heavenly Father. This is the dad Jesus identifies with, the dad he looks to for his identity and his mission in life. Jesus gains his strength, help, encouragement, and direction for what lies ahead from God the Father.

Jesus doesn't take his identity, cues, or affirmation from the masses. His sense of self isn't tied to his work, possessions, or power. Though he has the ability to miraculously restore limbs to lepers, give sight to the blind, and supply supersize baskets of loaves and fishes to large crowds, it's all in a day's work for Jesus. Everything he does flows out of his relationship with his Father. So close is this remarkable father-son relationship that Jesus tells Philip that whoever has seen him has seen the Father (John 14:9). Jesus' identity is anchored in the intimate knowledge that he is the beloved Son of his Father; his one and only passion in life is pleasing his Father. Everything Jesus is and everything Jesus does flows out of who he is as a chosen, loved, and accepted Son of God. And still, we don't hear God the Father say a whole lot to Jesus. The Gospels offer a few snapshots of Jesus waking up early, getting away from the multitudes, and going off alone to pray and talk with God. Conspicuously absent are the words shared between Father and Son. We don't get to eavesdrop on their intimate conversations. But we don't need to. What few words we hear God the Father speak to Jesus are all the words Jesus needs to hear. And at their core, these words are all we really need to know to discover whose children we are. Though Jesus grew up studying the Jewish law, he sums up the entire law in two commands: Love God and love others. Loving God and loving others is a clear mark of who Jesus knows himself to be as the loved and accepted Son of God. From this identity, Jesus lives a life of "keeping the main thing the main thing." Loving God and loving others is the evidence of a strong spiritual identity rooted in Christ.

> **Everything Jesus is and everything Jesus does flows out of who he is as a chosen, loved, and accepted Son of God.**

25

The same can be true for us: When we know whose we are, our lives can be marked with a deeper love for God and for others. This is the transforming life available to us as we discover our true identity as children of God. So why are there so many people who don't experience this transforming spiritual life? Why do so many people who claim to be followers of Jesus fear God the Father like he is ready to vaporize them for the slightest infraction? Why is the Christian life, for some, characterized by more guilt, frustration, shame, and confusion than the simple knowledge that our heavenly Father loves us as his children? As I mentioned in the previous chapter, I'm convinced that the longing in our heart goes back to the homes, classrooms, parks, and playgrounds where we grew up as kids. It's where we were named either by our fathers and mothers, others, or ourselves. Even in our churches, some of us have been named hurtful, damaging names. Names our hearts could do without.

Steven

One Saturday morning, Scott, a friend of mine, was standing in his driveway dinking around, not doing much of anything, when he eyed his neighbor's son Steven riding his bike. Steven was wearing his baseball uniform. My friend didn't know that Steven was on a baseball team or that he played competitive sports.

"Hey, Steven, what position do you play?"

Steven is a nice kid. Brown hair. Always ready with a funny joke or two. He sat there on his bike, not answering right away. His dad stood in the driveway. Like Steven, his dad is a joker. Works a lot. Talks a lot.

Unsure if Steven had heard him the first time, Scott raised his voice a little louder. "Hey, Steven, what position do you play?"

This time, Steven heard the question. He turned, looked at Scott, and began to say, "Second—" when his dad cut him off with a verbal pickoff. Steven's dad stood in the driveway and delivered the pitch. A razored barb coming in low and fast on the inside. His exact words were, "Splinter-picker."

Steven reeled, not knowing what to say, head hanging in shame. Scott's mouth dropped opened, gasping in amazement. *Did I just hear what I think I heard?*

Let's play it again. Listen to it with your heart in slow mo.

"Hey, Steven, what position do you play?"

Splinter-picker.

The dad tried to soften the blow with a laugh. He should write jokes for Leno.

What happens in the heart of a boy when his dad verbally ridicules him in front of another man? Steven was embarrassed. Scott said he was dumbstruck, not knowing what to say or do, though he did feel an acute impulse to go back inside his home, grab a baseball bat, and hold an impromptu "come to Jesus" meeting.

Is it any wonder that sarcasm, as the Greeks defined it, means "to tear flesh"? How long will Steven be picking splinters stuck deep in his heart? It makes me wonder how Steven's father was named by his father. When did the barbs begin?

I wish Steven's baseball experience had been more positive, like mine. The Philadelphia Phillies was my first Little League baseball team. My five sisters got a lot of mileage teasing me for being on a team named after a herd of female horses. Though my sisters teased me, at least I didn't have to ride the bench. I now know that the correct spelling for a female horse is "filly," so even though I had to endure for an entire season of being on a second-grade team of female horses, I didn't care because I got to play every game.

Our first season was a banner year. We went 0—10. Go Phillies.

Despite our complete lack of athletic ability and hardcore competitive edge to slaughter our opponents, I discovered in that first season of baseball that my father's love wasn't dependent on whether I won or lost, whether I hit home runs or cried after striking out. He just showed up for the games, which is a lot more than the dads of many men I've spoken to who are grieving in their thirties and forties because their dads never came to their athletic events or school functions. There is a long leash tied to the longing in our hearts and the truth that some of our parents were never there for us.

There was the time, though, a day I'll never forget, when I hit two home runs in one game. That's right; I clobbered two not-so-fastballs right out of the park over that massive, three-foot-high green cloth fence 150 feet from home plate. Hitting one home run was great—the dream of every kid who stands at the plate and stares down the pitcher—but when that second ball soared over the outfield fence and I threw down the bat on my way to first base, you should have heard my father's voice: *Ya-hooo!*

As our team's bench cleared to meet me at home plate, my dad had a smile on his face the size of third base, yelling and rejoicing along with the rest of my teammates. What dad doesn't love seeing his kid hit a homer? What child doesn't crave the look of pure pleasure of pleasing his or her father? And that's part of the longing too; we all hunger to please our fathers and we long to hear our fathers cheer us on.

As a child, you looked to your mother and father, your brothers and sisters for identity, to gain a sense of who you were in relationship to them and the world around you. What you were named shaped your understanding of where you stand in relation to those around you. How were you named by your father or mother? Did your father or mother spend more time chewing you out than cheering you on? Were you called "splinter-picker" or did your father look you in the eye and say in a proud voice, "Good job, son." Was your home filled with more criticism than encouragement?

> Our spiritual identity, how we see ourselves in relationship to God and one another, is directly tied to how we have been named in the past and how we accept ourselves based on who God says we are as his children.

These are simple questions, and they shouldn't take long to answer. If we hesitate in answering them with a resounding yes or a definitive no, we show our ambivalence and reveal hearts that wonder where we really stand. If we were given the precious gift of being loved and accepted, we'd speak from a secure, confident heart, wouldn't we? Regardless of who named us, what we have been named plays a powerful role in shaping how we see ourselves as children of God. Our spiritual identity, how we see ourselves in relationship to God and one another, is directly tied to how we have been named in the past and how we accept ourselves based on who God says we are as his children. This is where you and I could use Jesus' help. How he was named by his Father can lead us to the place of discovering our true identity as sons and daughters of God.

God Goes Public

Toward the end of Jesus' three-year ministry, immediately before he lets his disciples in on the secret that he is going to suffer and be handed over to death, Jesus takes Peter, James, and John on a hike to the top of a mountain, where he is transfigured in dazzling white before them. If there was ever a mountaintop experience, this was it. Elijah and Moses show up to talk with Jesus; what they talk about is known only to eternity.

While Jesus huddles with Elijah and Moses, Peter, James, and John are hunkered down in absolute terror. When the light show around Jesus ends, a lightbulb clicks on in Peter's brain. What if, Peter suggests to Jesus in a stroke of Peter-esque brilliance, they all set up camp instead of heading down the mountain where the mere mortals dwell? Jesus, Moses, and Elijah each could get their own tent, and Peter, James, and John could hang with the spiritual heavyweights. In the three Gospel accounts of this story, the weather changes, the whole group is enveloped in a cloud, and God interrupts Peter with a heavenly "ahem." God has a different agenda in mind, namely the redemption of the world. God has words for Jesus. And for Peter.

While Peter was still speaking, a bright cloud enveloped them, and a voice from the cloud said, "This is my Son, whom I love; with him I am well pleased. Listen to him!" (Matt. 17:5).

What do Jesus and the disciples hear from the clouds? The voice of God. And what kinds of words come from that voice? Words of relationship and belonging. Closeness and connection. Intimacy and security. Affection and affirmation. Acceptance and assurance. Confidence and strength. Truth and tender love. Words that tell us to listen.

We see God the Father telling Jesus and everyone near him exactly who he is.

This is my Son, whom I love, and in whom I take great pleasure.

Jesus has been named by his Father, and what Jesus is named makes all the difference in the world in who he understands himself to be and what God has called him to do. At his baptism before the beginning of his ministry, Jesus is affirmed for who he is as God's Son. At his transfiguration at the end of his ministry, Jesus receives the confirmation of the Father's great pleasure in him. Affirmation and confirmation are present at two of the most critical moments in Jesus' life.

> Without that *name*, without that *voice*, we are left to wonder who we are and what we will become.

Isn't this what you longed for as a child and perhaps are still longing for as an adult? When was the last time someone affirmed you for who you are and confirmed their great pleasure in you? Every child has key moments when they need to hear the love, affirmation, and confirmation of who they are. Without that *name*, without that *voice*, we are left to wonder who we are and what we will become. Names mean something. Who doesn't want to be named something good and positive?

Do the Math

Tears pouring down his cheeks, my seven-year-old son, Joseph Allen O'Connor IV, sat at our kitchen table in emotional shambles. His first-grade homework assignment was to find out the meaning of his name. A couple years ago, Joseph, Aidan, and I gave each other nicknames for our backyard adventures and wrestling matches. Joseph is "Hunter." Aidan is "Scout." I am "Soldier."

With a nickname like Hunter, Joseph envisioned his real name worthy of fierce battles and extraordinary expeditions. At least something along the lines of "ant killer." So when my wife looked in a baby name book and told Joseph the real meaning of his fourth generation family name, Joseph discovered, to his first-grade angst, that his name means "he shall add."

He cried, "That's not cool! That's like math!"

Joseph buried his face in his arms on the kitchen table, foreseeing a dismal future, forever named Joseph the Bank Teller or Joseph the Bean Counter. Not knowing he was throwing salt into his own wound, Joseph asked Krista to look up the meaning of his friend's name, Mark.

Krista scanned the page and responded to Joseph's inquiry.

"Mark means 'warlike.'"

That did not help. Wisely discerning the identity crisis at hand, Krista tore through the name book. "Well, let's see what your middle name means."

> Do the math for yourself. How you have been named and how often you heard specific names throughout the course of your life has so much to do with how you see yourself.

She flipped through a couple pages. "Allen means 'handsome and cheerful.'"

Joseph perked up. Now his name was in line with a debonair lady-killer. He liked the idea of being called handsome, and since his temperament is easygoing and cheerful, his new names were consistent with how he saw himself. Krista had his attention. "Let's look up the name Connor," she said, turning a couple more pages. "Connor means 'wise aid.'" Joseph smiled. A minute before, he thought his name would forever peg him as an integer-loving mathematician, but now he saw himself as handsome, cheerful, and wise.

Do the math for yourself. How you have been named and how often you have heard specific names throughout the course of your life has so much to do with how you see yourself. And we do become what we see, don't we? Much of our identity is formed and shaped by the cumulative sum of what others have named us and the traumas that have given us names we never asked for. Confidence flows out of confirmation. Self-acceptance is the fruit born out of being affirmed and accepted by others. Security is the safety we feel to be at home in our hearts in spite of what others may say to hurt us.

What names drift through the hearts and minds of victims of sexual abuse? *Dirty. Secret. Hidden in darkness.* What about the child who never received praise or acceptance from a father or mother? *Unworthy. Lazy. Loser.* Or the child who grew up in a chaotic, violent home, not knowing what a healthy relationship is? *Scattered. Scared. Not able to trust.* Or the child whose mother or father left home with or without explanation? *Alone. Abandoned. Unloved.* From the names and wounds of childhood come the quiet, fear-filled voices that whisper:

After all you've done, what makes you think God will forgive you?

People have let you down all your life. Trust no one.

Don't be vulnerable. Hide your true feelings.

Don't appear weak, or people will walk all over you.

Our family has never done that. Settle for less and lower your expectations.

If you screw up, people won't accept you.

Suck it up . . . you're the only one who feels this way.

Win at all costs. Losing confirms you're a loser.

Your inability to make something of your life proves your worthlessness.

If people knew the real you, they'd be out of your life in a heartbeat.

You'll never amount to much. What makes you think you can do that?

35

You are ugly and unlovable. Get over it and accept your
    lot in life.

You are a dirty, sinful person. Work hard to prove your-
    self worthy.

After eighteen years of ministry, the past five spent
working with adults and families in grief recovery,
I've discovered that the condemning voices, wound-
ing words, and emotional names we've experienced
in childhood wreak untold damage in the heart of all
of us who long to hear the simple, transforming message that we are chosen, loved, and accepted by God.
These are the voices I've heard flowing out of people's
hearts, words that they have never had the permission
or safety to say out loud. For far too long, they have
seen the world through a fog of grief and unresolved
wounds, not knowing that they are looking through the
scratched lens of a broken heart.

It is through the eyes and hearts of our fathers and
mothers, how they viewed us, interacted with us, and
dealt with us that we receive our lens for the world. The
primary task of adulthood and growing in Christ is to
stop, take off the glasses, see the scars and scratches for
what they are, and begin looking through the lens God
offers us through our new birth in Christ. We can only
grow in Christ to the degree that we are looking through
the same lens God is, so that we can rightly see ourselves
from his vantage point.

How many of us are unaware that the lens our parents gave us is the same lens through which we see God? Is it any wonder that we have a slight tendency to create God the Father in the image of our parents? We forever feel distant, angry, and ambivalent toward God, even though intellectually we know we're supposed to love him, just like we're supposed to love our parents. How do you see God the Father? As a dad who chooses, loves, and accepts you? An understanding dad? A caring dad? A spineless dad? A do-whatever-you-want, permissive dad? A cynical dad? An absent dad? A workaholic dad? Or Dad the Drinker? Dad the Control Freak? Dad the Womanizer? Dad the Rager?

Cassandra

Cassandra and her husband, Jason, came to my office several times for marriage counseling. Both were young, and Cassandra complained about Jason's inability to meet her emotional needs. "I want him to tell me I'm beautiful and sexy. I want him to notice me." And so Jason and I talked. He readily acknowledged that he didn't do emotions very well and that he was raised in an emotionally frigid home where no one knew how to express warmth and affection. Yes, he could be controlling at times, and he was sorry for hurting Cassandra's feelings. Jason took responsibility for his part in their marriage struggles and was very willing to learn new ways to meet his wife's emotional needs.

When I asked Cassandra about her relationship with her father, she replied that she was raised in a Christian home in which she was loved by both her parents. At first mention, Cassandra said her dad was loving, caring, and supportive. But as the three of us talked more about her father, a completely different picture emerged. What surfaced was a snapshot of a workaholic father who was controlling and physically abusive toward her mother. Cassandra's father had shown her little in the way of physical affection or verbal affirmation.

Cassandra's longing for a loving, caring, and supportive father was the same longing she wanted her husband to fill. Yet Cassandra wanted to make Jason the sole source of their marriage problems. It was now Jason's job to fill the emotional hole in her heart left by her father, a hole no human could completely fill. She couldn't trust Jason because she couldn't trust her father or any other man she had ever met. But she couldn't see how her father's neglect had played a part in her unrealistic ideals for Jason. Expecting a husband or wife to fill the gaping longing in our heart that only God can fill is like trying to duct tape the Titanic.

What keeps husbands and wives from seeing and respecting one another? What keeps some single adults in a perpetual spin of negative, abusive relationships? How often do we agonize over the "issues" in our relationships instead of understanding that the core problem goes back to the longing of not being chosen, loved, or accepted as children? Instead of looking at some of our wounds that have been with us for many years, it's much easier to look at our spouse's flaws and try to fix or control them. It's always easier to fix someone else instead of ourselves, isn't it?

How was Cassandra named by her father? Yes, she had definite marriage problems, but her underlying problem, her real issue, was the core wound in her heart dealt by her father years before she ever met Jason. Until this wound from her father was addressed, there wasn't much hope for resolving her conflicts with Jason.

It is no understatement to say that how our parents shaped us and influenced the development of our identity plays a significant role in how we view ourselves and, ultimately, how we view our heavenly Father. Our capacity to receive the truth that we are loved children of God is largely dependent on how we are able to reflect on our relationships with our earthly fathers. We have to compassionately sift out the truth that our fathers and mothers too were once children who longed to be loved by their fathers and mothers. And with the help of the Holy Spirit, we need to humbly receive the truth of who God the Father says we really are as his children.

It is through the eyes and heart of our heavenly Father that we can begin to see, every day, our lives with whole new eyes. Seeing ourselves and one another as God the Father sees us, again, is a question of spiritual identity. Knowing whose we are will transform how we see our fathers and mothers as well as silence the voices of the past that say we are anything less than the chosen, loved, and accepted children of God.

It is from our heavenly Father that we learn to trust again and discover our true worth as children of God. If you have trouble with the idea of trusting a loving, heavenly Father, you are not alone. *Father* is a terrifying word for many people. But what if I were to introduce you to a whole new Father? A Father completely different than the father you've known here on earth. This is the Father who notices you. The Father who chooses, loves, and accepts you. Psalm 145 introduces you and me to a Father who, unlike Cassandra's dad or perhaps your dad, has the kind of incredible character qualities that every child needs. It's never too late for you to have a whole new Father.

> The LORD is gracious and compassionate,
> *(God's grace and compassion for you is without measure*
> *or limit.)*
> slow to anger and rich in love (v. 8).
> *(God will never scream or rage at you. This Father has a*
> *wealth of love for you.)*
> The LORD is good to all;
> *(That includes you. Even when you blow it and mess up.)*
> he has compassion on all he has made (v. 9).
> *(God won't come down on you like an angry parent.*
> *His compassion comes on you.)*
> The LORD is faithful to all his promises
> *(Ever had a dad who didn't keep promises? Not this one.*
> *God is always faithful.)*
> and loving toward all he has made (v. 13).

(God sees you. He knows you. He loves you. He notices you.)
The LORD upholds all those who fall
and lifts up all who are bowed down (v. 14).

In your brokenness and failings, God promises to lift you up and hold you up.

A father of grace and compassion. A father who is slow to anger and rich in love. A father who is good to all and who has compassion on all his children. A father who shows up, keeps his promises, and is loving toward all he has made. Last, God is a father who picks up his kids when they fall down. A dad who lifts his children up and cradles them in his arms of love. This is your true Father.

THREE

You Are Immensely Worth Saving

One Sunday afternoon I took two of my children, Ellie and Joseph, and two of our friend's children, Billy and Mary, to the San Juan Capistrano Mission. Named the "Jewel of the California Missions," the mission has become in recent years one of my favorite places to spend time alone with God. From the beautiful gardens to small chapels filled with warm, glowing candles to quiet, bubbling fountains to the ruins of the Great Stone Church, the mission offers me many places to steal away. It's one of those sacred places needed in the life of every person whose longing in the heart is never sated by the world's flavor of the day. The mission is where I go to recalibrate my heart. To remind myself whose I really am. To detach from the self-inflicting talons of narcissism that come with trying to be CEO of my life.

Today was not one of those days.

By an unintentional stroke of insanity, we had eight kids staying with us that weekend. Four of our own and a 3 + 1 combination plate from two other families. To keep our neighbors from calling the police for disturbing the peace, I took this foursome to the mission because my kids love to play there. When I was a kid, my dad took me to the mission to feed the pigeons, and now I find great pleasure watching my kids tear around the gardens, check out the guns and swords in the soldiers' barracks, visit the spooky graveyard, and attempt to fish like grizzlies by swiping at the koi fish in the fountains. But where my kids really love to go, like all kids, is the gift store.

Like any other self-respecting parent who knows how to handle four kids in a tourist gift store filled with glass items, I firmly told the kids not to touch anything. I should have said nothing. Just mentioning the *T* word guarantees that something is going to get broken. As the kids were scurrying from aisle to aisle looking at all the mission merchandise, I stood at the cash register to ask a question. I had my back to the store.

Immediately behind me, a sharp, high-pitched crash pierced the air. I whipped around, and there stood six-year-old Mary next to a shelf filled with small glass sparrows. The same fragile, breakable glass sparrows found in every gift store, that chirp in a soft whisper to vulnerable six-year-olds, "Touch me! Touch me! Touch me!" And the second that little glass bird convinces the unsuspecting child to pick it up, it suddenly finds its wings and crashes to the hard Mexican tiles below.

Broken glass lay at Mary's feet. Her eyes darted and locked on mine in a stunned silence. We were both thinking the same thing: *Oh, crud.* The two women at the cash register glared at Mary with laser-beam eyes. I felt my blood begin to rise, because I had exercised a great deal of restraint toward all the kids by not chanting the gift store mantra: "Nice to touch. Nice to hold. If you break it, consider it sold." I didn't touch the little glass sparrow and I didn't break it, but now I was going to be the one to pay for it.

Mary stood frozen next to the bird shelf. I knelt down next to her, and when our eyes met again, I could tell she was embarrassed and afraid. She knew she was in trouble. She could feel it coming. Somebody was ready to unload on her. She was about to get doubled-teamed by the cashier ladies, me, or worse, all three of us, for breaking that little sparrow. Bird breaking is a serious mission infraction. It's even against the law in San Juan to keep swallows from nesting in the eaves of your home, let alone break one in the gift shop.

Now, in crisis situations like this, my normal reaction is to unload and reload, especially after I have just told everyone not to touch anything. But in that split second when

Mary's and my eyes met, by a gift of grace, God helped me see a scared child instead of a broken bird. I knelt down next to Mary, looked her in the eyes, and said in a soft voice just between her and me, "That's okay, Mary. You didn't mean to break the bird. It was just an accident."

"I didn't mean to do it," Mary agreed. "It *was* just an accident."

"I know. That's all it was. Just an accident."

I gave her a little hug and started picking up the pieces. I took the broken merchandise to the cashier and awkwardly said that I would pay for it. The lady gave a short smile and shook her head. "No, really, I can," I insisted. Both of the ladies shook their heads and said, "That's okay."

Later that night in the kitchen as we were getting dinner ready for our pack of wolves, I mean, the eight kids, Mary and I relayed the broken sparrow story to Krista. As we recounted the details of the story, Mary said to me, "I felt embarrassed. That lady just stared at me." Even though no one unloaded on Mary with a harsh scolding, she knew the spotlight was on her and she felt the heat of the woman's glare. Even though breaking the sparrow was just an accident, Mary felt the hot sting of embarrassment and the brand it left on her heart.

Your True Worth

Do you ever have days when you feel like Mary? You feel like God is glaring at you. You blew it again, and now you've really ticked him off. His lips are pursed in an uptight snarl, and he's ready to unload on you for causing another accident. Or maybe it wasn't even an accident. You did something wrong, and you knew exactly what you were doing. You broke something. Again. You wish it was something as insignificant as a glass sparrow. Broken pieces lay all around you. Your marriage. Your kids. Or maybe you're single, and you view your singleness as a punishment. Your work and friendships aren't what they used to be. Your life feels like an accident. One huge cosmic mistake. You feel like you have to apologize constantly for who you are and what you do. Or don't do. You figure that forgiveness can only go so far. Grace has got to stop somewhere. Mercy is meant for people who make good on their promises to God.

And so you stay frozen. You're waiting for booming thunder and flashing lightning to unload from the dark skies of heaven. You're waiting for the deafening sound that sounds vaguely familiar: "I can't believe you did it again! Can't you do anything right? Didn't I tell you not to touch anything?" You're waiting for condemnation. And so you don't touch anything. And you won't let anything get near enough to touch you. Why wait around to hear who God says you are when you already have a very clear view of who you are, right?

Wrong. For too long now, your heart has heard more condemnation than the truth of your chosenness. Maybe you've experienced more law than love in the church. You're far more familiar with accusation than

47

acceptance. And so what do you do? Instead of finding freedom in the unconditional love and forgiveness offered in Jesus Christ, your heart slams into a wall of condemnation. In a warped distortion of grace, you listen to lying whispers instead of God's loving voice affirming your chosenness. You live under the weight of legalistic religion defined by do's and don'ts instead of the embrace of God's kindness.

> Right now, this very instant, if you are a child of God in Christ, you are not condemned.

But wait. All those voices you hear in your head and heart—are they really God speaking, or does he have something else to say? Despite all the broken sparrows, all the shattered glass around your feet, who does God say you really are?

If I were stranded on a deserted island like Tom Hanks in *Cast Away,* and I could rip out only one chapter in the Bible to read, without a doubt, I would choose chapter 8 in the book of Romans. Verse 1 opens with the amazing promise of God: "Therefore, there is now no condemnation for those who are in Christ Jesus." Right now, this very instant, if you are a child of God in Christ, you are not condemned. It doesn't matter what voices you've heard, how others have hurt you in the past, the mistakes you made last week, or how you wish you were a better or stronger or more loving person instead of the fickle, temperamental, grumpy person you can be—right now, there is no condemnation for you in Christ Jesus. His love for you isn't dependent on what you do but on who you are as his child.

Romans 8 ends with the promise that there is nothing that can separate you from the love of God that is offered to you through Christ Jesus. As John Piper wrote in *Knowing God*, Romans 8 begins with "no condemnation" and ends with "no separation." In Christ, your past, present, and future have been forgiven. In Christ, you are not condemned, you *cannot* be condemned, and nothing can separate you from the love of God. In between, we are given the promises of God that we are his sons and daughters and that he is our *abba*, our daddy who graciously gives us the Holy Spirit, our comforter and friend who helps us live whole new lives as the children of God. If you've felt like you live under more condemnation than the loving grace of God, you're not alone. If you think you're not a very good Christian, Jesus would love to spend some time with you.

The people who pretended to be good were the same people who had problems with Jesus. One day, Jesus was speaking to two groups of people. Group #1, the Pharisees, considered themselves to be very religious. Very tight with God. The other group, Jesus' disciples and the crowd that followed, weren't exactly the church-going type. They weren't very religious. They were more aware of their own brokenness, and they were hungry and thirsty for something more than living by the harsh standards of the law. Seeing that Group #2 was quite intimidated by Group #1, Jesus said, "Are not five sparrows sold for two pennies? Yet not one of them is forgotten by God. Indeed, the very hairs of your head are all numbered. Don't be afraid; you are worth more than many sparrows" (Luke 12:6–7).

In God's eyes you are worth more than many sparrows; but even greater than that, God knows you so intimately that he has already counted the hairs on your head. Just as you might run your fingers through the hair of one of your children, marveling at how they grow, God offers you his loving affection as a Father. If not a single sparrow in this world is forgotten by God, Jesus says, then his Father will never forget you. Your value as a chosen child of God is incomparable to the seemingly smallest and insignificant parts of his creation. Your truth worth is in God and from God because he created you for the purpose of knowing and enjoying him.

> Until your heart finds its rest in God alone, you will never experience the peace your heart longs for.

St. Augustine wrote, "You move us to delight in praising You; for You have formed us for Yourself, and our hearts are restless till they find rest in You." The whole course of your life is a search for being chosen, loved, and accepted. *This is the longing.* God chooses you, loves you, and accepts you. Until your heart finds its rest in God alone, you will never experience the peace your heart longs for. Your heart is longing for God, and you may not even know it. In Psalm 84, the psalmist writes that his heart and everything in him longs to find its true home in God.

> My soul yearns, even faints,
>   for the courts of the LORD;
> my heart and my flesh cry out
>   for the living God.

> Even the sparrow has found a home,
>   and the swallow a nest for herself,
>   where she may have her young—
> a place near your altar,
>   O LORD Almighty, my King and my God.
>
> Psalm 84:2–3

If God can provide a home for the sparrow and the swallow near his altar, he certainly has room enough for you. Read Psalm 139 and discover how intimately God knows and loves you. David praises God because he has found the source of his true value. Discovering that his life has meaning and value and purpose to God, David writes:

> For you created my inmost being;
>   you knit me together in my mother's womb.
> I praise you because I am fearfully and wonderfully
>   made;
>   your works are wonderful,
>   I know that full well.
>
> Psalm 139:13–14

51

Baby Steps

Maybe you're reading this book and find that the whole idea of being a chosen, loved, and accepted child of God is absolutely foreign to you. You're a little leery with all this talk about an unmet longing. Perhaps you're intrigued with the idea that there's someone who sees beyond your brokenness and loves you far beyond your wildest imagination. For as long as you can remember, you've longed for someone to remove the heavy cloud hanging over your heart, to rip off what seems to be a heavy canvas tarp covering the real you. You felt the tender tug of God pulling on your heart, but no one has shown you the next step. In order to discover whose you really are and who you were made to be, the first step of your spiritual journey must be to actually become a child of God. But to take that first step, we need to eliminate some confusion about what it means to be a child of God.

A lot of popular thinking today is based on the assumption that being born on this earth automatically makes you a child of God. If you believe in God, that gives you the inherent right to be a child of God, right? Sounds good, but not exactly. The Bible tells a different story. In God's eyes, there are two types of children: children of Adam and children of God. We are all born separated from God through the sin of Adam, and we become the sons and daughters of God through the saving work of Jesus Christ.

To truly understand the depth of what it means to be chosen, loved, and accepted, we must deal with the problem of sin. If we don't deal with sin as Scripture does, the fact that God chooses us in spite of our sin doesn't mean much. Dallas Willard writes in *Renovation of the Heart*, "Even in its ruined condition a human being is regarded by God as something immensely worth saving. Sin does not make it worthless, but only lost. And in its lostness it is still capable of great strength, dignity, and heartbreaking beauty and goodness."[4]

Think about that: God loves you so much that he sees your life as immensely worth saving. In Christ you go from death to life. From being separated to being chosen. From the ugliness of sin to being affectionately loved. From rejection to acceptance. From a longing to a life-transforming love. Paul writes, "Death initially came by a man, and resurrection from death came by a man. Everybody dies in Adam; everybody comes alive in Christ" (1 Cor. 15:21–22 Message). It is only by the shed blood of Christ that we move from being children of Adam under sin, the law, and death, to being adopted children into the family of God, which brings us freedom, hope, and life. Becoming a son or daughter of God is based on receiving and believing in the name of Jesus. John writes, "Yet to all who received him, to those who believed in his name, he gave the right to become children of God—children born not of natural descent, nor of human decision or a husband's will, but born of God" (John 1:12–13).

In John 3, a man named Nicodemus came to Jesus in the middle of the night to talk with him about spiritual life. Jesus told Nicodemus that no one could see or know what the kingdom of God is all about unless they are born again. Very clearly, he made a sharp distinction between physical birth and spiritual birth. Jesus also told Nicodemus the exact purpose of his mission on earth, which was to offer eternal life, not a crusade of condemnation. Jesus came to choose, love, and accept all who were alienated from God. "For God so loved the world that he gave his one and only Son, that whoever believes in him shall not perish but have eternal life. For God did not send his Son into the world to condemn the world, but to save the world through him" (John 3:16–17). Your life is worth saving, and the good news of the gospel is that you don't have to try to save yourself.

How many people are on a relentless search to save themselves through developing a positive self-image and propping themselves up with constant reminders that they are "good" people? Countless books, tapes, and seminars are available to help you and me develop a high self-esteem. There's nothing wrong with feeling good about ourselves, and I don't want to beat up the broken, because insecurity and self-hatred are first born out of our separation from God, and second, by others' inability or unwillingness to love. But if you really want to develop an accurate view of who you are, you must first understand whose image you are made in. You are called to something so much higher than a good self-esteem. You are called and made to reflect the very image of God! If you really understand that you are made in the image of God, and that in Christ the broken image of the fall is restored, then all the questions of self-esteem eventually fall by the wayside.

When you know you're loved, you don't obsess about a positive self-image or rate your self-esteem from day to day like a Gallup opinion poll. You don't base your understanding of who you are on the fickle opinions of others. You no longer live under the tyranny of praise, acceptance, fear, or rejection of others. In Christ, you see yourself as God sees you. Chosen. Loved. Accepted. Forgiven. Whole. Holy.

You are called to something so much higher than high self-esteem. You are called and made to reflect the very image of God!

Jesus said if you want to find your life, first lose it through loving God and loving others. By losing yourself, you will find yourself.

> If anyone would come after me, he must deny himself and take up his cross and follow me. For whoever wants to save his life will lose it, but whoever loses his life for me will find it. What good will it be for a man if he gains the whole world, yet forfeits his soul? Or what can a man give in exchange for his soul?
>
> Matthew 16:24–26

When you stop trying to save yourself by meditating on self-esteem mantras or staying on Santa's "nice" list, and instead allow God's love to free you from incessant self-preoccupation, you will begin to see yourself as God sees you. You will see that he loves you for just being you. You will begin to relax in whose you are by finding your ultimate meaning, purpose, and significance in who God says you are. Ultimately, how you see yourself or how others see you will no long matter.

You are born once when you pop out of your mother's birth canal. You are born again when your heart experiences spiritual rebirth in Christ through the forgiveness of the sins that formerly separated you from God. Paul affirms John's words by writing, "You are all sons [and daughters] of God through faith in Christ Jesus" (Gal. 3:26). We become sons and daughters of God through faith in Christ, which is a free gift from God. This free gift comes through the unconditional love, grace, and mercy of God. In his letter to the people in the town of Ephesus, Paul writes, "For it is by grace you have been saved, through faith—and this not from yourselves, it is the gift of God—not by works, so that no one can boast" (Eph. 2:8–9).

You cannot earn, purchase, or win the right to become a child of God in your own power and strength. I can't. You can't. Your spouse and children can't. Your co-workers and friends can't. You and I aren't chosen, loved, and accepted because of our talents and abilities, the family we were born into, the church we attended when we grew up, or how often we volunteer in our community. We don't earn God's favor by our good works, how much money we donate, or how nice we are to our neighbors. Nice is not enough. Dallas Willard writes, "I'm *not* okay and you're *not* okay. We're all in serious trouble."[5]

Our sin stands in the way of God, and it is the perfect sacrifice of Jesus on the cross that God provides as the only way for us to make our peace with him. "Therefore, since we have been justified through faith, we have peace with God through our Lord Jesus Christ, through whom we have gained access by faith into this grace in which we now stand" (Rom. 5:1–2). It is through and by faith, essentially saying yes to God, that we gain access into the gift of grace to stand as children in the loving presence of God the Father.

Faith. Grace. Love. The cross of Christ.

All are gifts.

Gifts from your Father calling you as one who is chosen, loved, and accepted.

If no one has ever told you how to start a whole new friendship with God, your first step is to receive God's unconditional love and forgiveness through Jesus Christ. And that's a baby step you can take today. All you need to do is say yes to what God has already provided for you in Christ. Once you take this life-transforming step, you will begin to see the growth of your true spiritual identity.

Beginning Your Whole New Childhood Today

Whether you have been a traveler along the Way for many years or have found this book to be your first personal introduction to living as a child of God, every day ahead offers you the opportunity to live a whole new childhood. Whether you have fond memories of your childhood or not, living as a child of God begins with receiving his kingdom, his loving rule in your life, with the faith of a child. God has a second childhood in store for everyone who is willing to listen to the words of Jesus: "I tell you the truth, unless you change and become like little children, you will never enter the kingdom of heaven" (Matt. 18:3).

Have you ever stopped to watch a child eat a bowl of cereal? Watching my four-year-old sit and eat a bowl of Rice Chex is a lesson in living in the moment. Completely focused in the now, Aidan only cares about chasing that little soggy square around a blue bowl with his Winnie the Pooh spoon. As he goes for another scoop, his slurping is the sound of aliveness. Pure pleasure. Jesus reminds us adults that we have a lot to learn by becoming children. Mark writes:

> People were bringing little children to Jesus to have him touch them, but the disciples rebuked them. When Jesus saw this, he was indignant. He said to them, "Let the little children come to me, and do not hinder them, for the kingdom of God belongs to such as these. I tell you the truth, anyone who will not receive the kingdom of God like a little child will never enter it." And he took the children in his arms, put his hands on them and blessed them.
>
> Mark 10:13–16

Jesus doesn't want anything or anyone to hinder you from receiving the blessing of his unconditional love. By receiving his kingdom with the faith of a child, you enter into a whole new childhood marked by love, joy, peace, patience, kindness, goodness, faithfulness, gentleness, and self-control. This is the fruit of Holy Spirit, the evidence of God at work, produced by everyone who is a child of God.

Your true worth is found in him. Even if you have been a wild and reckless prodigal running away from God, God still pursues you with the relentless love of a father. A father unlike any father you've never known. If you've spent your life trying to measure your worth by your career or your possessions, you need to know that God's love for you is priceless. It's absolutely free, so you can never puff up with pride by saying you paid your own way.

Maybe you've battled addictions and find it next to impossible to stay clean—as a child of God you'll be glad to know this is one family you'll never get kicked out of. Or maybe you're buried in grief, mourning a loss so overwhelming that the thought of making it through today seems as difficult as pushing a boulder uphill underwater—as a child of God you'll find that Jesus offers to lighten your load. All these and many more are the free gifts God offers to his children. John, named by Jesus as "the beloved disciple," writes from firsthand experience, "How great is the love the Father has lavished on us, that we should be called children of God! And that is what we are!" (1 John 3:1).

To find your true voice, your identity rooted in the tender, relentless love of God, you have to first understand what God says about you . . . the real you . . . the true you. And the evidence for who you really are as a child of God is quite conclusive. In the chapter that follows, I invite you to sit down and listen carefully to who God says you are through the timeless truths of his Word. Search through the pages of Scripture, and you will find the words of God affirming who you are as his child. Listen to these words. Meditate on them. Commit them to memory. Let them linger in your heart and thoughts throughout the day. They offer you the transforming truth to see with new eyes how God sees you and who he says you are.

For years people have been telling you who you are and what you should be, but what matters most in this life is who God says you are. You are worth more than many sparrows. Your life is far more valuable than you realize. No matter what you've been through or what you are going through right now, your life is immensely worth saving. Even if it's broken. Your life is not an accident, and here's why . . .

FOUR

God Is for You

Last summer, my thirteen-year-old daughter, Janae, and I went to Mexico to work at an orphanage for the weekend. When we pulled into the orphanage, I noticed it was quite unlike any orphanage I'd ever visited in Mexico. Nestled in a small valley south of Rosarito Beach, Puerta de Fe (Door of Faith) sat among beautiful sycamore and pepper trees. Brilliant bougainvillea draped a historic hunting lodge on premises that used to entertain Clark Gable and John Wayne. The whole facility, which is home to over a hundred orphans, ranging in age from six-month-old infants to eighteen-year-old students, was clean and inviting.

Along with thirty other middle school students, our team got busy painting walls, pouring cement, and playing with the children. Behind the smiles of the children, though, were stories to chill the heart. One young boy had seen his brother shot to death. Many of the children had suffered physical and sexual abuse. Several of the infants were the victims of fetal alcohol syndrome or drug abuse. On the day we arrived, the orphanage received an eight-month-old baby. The Mexican authorities had even brought one baby who was almost sold on the black market on the Internet.

As I stood over the crib of a baby girl with fetal alcohol syndrome, tears welled up in my eyes as I wondered quietly, *Lord, why her and not me? How is it that I was born in America and not here? Why is this baby in the orphanage and not me?*

When I walked out of the nursery and into the courtyard, I was so overwhelmed with emotion that I could barely hold back my tears. I wondered what it really would be like to be an orphan. To always have a deep longing to be chosen. To wonder why I was rejected. What would it be like to go to bed alone, always longing for a mother? A father. A family.

No Longer Orphans

The baby girl in the orphanage was a living picture of discarded innocence. Her mother was not for her. Her father was not for her. Society was not for her. Despite the overwhelming obstacles ahead of her in life, one thing and one thing only is true: *God is for her*. Psalm 56:9 says, "This I know, that God is for me." Hopefully, through the love and compassion of the Christians running the orphanage, this baby girl will grow in the truth that God is for her. Despite her circumstances or the future implications of fetal alcohol syndrome, God is for this little girl. God is for her just as God is for you.

The questions I was asking at the orphanage weren't so different from the questions we ask when we live apart from God and who he is inviting us to be as children in his family. When we don't live with a deep understanding that God is for us, that his relentless love pursues us every morning when we wake up, our identity is quickly shaped by what others have named us or what we have named ourselves through our life experience of successes and defeats. We hear the nagging insecurities in other people's words or even in our own words when

When we don't live with a deep understanding that God is for us, that his relentless love pursues us every morning when we wake up, our identity is quickly shaped by what others have named us or what we have named ourselves through our life experience of successes and defeats.

we talk about ourselves with a critical self-assessment. When we look at ourselves in the mirror, we're tempted to live on the polar extremes of inflated egos or defeating self-hatred. If we're not careful to listen for that other Voice, we will spend our days living with divided hearts. Divided from ourselves. Divided from those trying to get close to us. Divided from God.

Unless we know *whose* we really are, we will live like orphans who've long given up the dream of ever being chosen, loved, and accepted by another. When we don't accept the truth that God is for us and do everything possible through the power he gives us to live from the center of this truth, our lives are marked by loneliness and isolation even in the midst of many relationships. What we are missing is the key relationship—a personal, intimate relationship with the God who is always for us.

Separated from God and left to our own devices, we are all spiritual orphans. It is only through Jesus Christ that we are adopted into the family of God. Our spiritual adoption is the beginning of discovering whose we really are. The Scriptures make very clear the state of our orphaned hearts apart from Christ. Yet even as children of God, we sometimes live with prodigal hearts. We run from relationship with God, seeking those things we think will ultimately satisfy us but never do. Just like the prodigal son, we end up eating out of the pigsty of our own illusions when we could be eating prime rib at home with our Father. When we come to our senses, that's when we journey home.

And every time, proving he is the loving Father that is always for us, God throws a party. With a relentless love we will never fathom, he sees us coming from a long way off. He calls out our true name—*chosen . . . loved . . . accepted*. He trades the rags of our rebellion for a fine robe and ring for our finger. Instead of punishment and condemnation, he slaughters the fatted calf and holds a feast in our honor. Though we act like runaways, he calls us—*my son . . . my daughter*. Though we sometimes live as orphans unwilling to believe that God's love is truly as unfailing as he says it is, our heavenly Father is patiently persistent to prove what so many others have been unable to in our life. God is always reaching out for us. Always coming to us. Always for us. How do we know this? Jesus, the chosen, loved, and accepted Son of God, shows us the way to the Father by promising to always be with us.

Immediately before his death, as he sat around the table with his disciples at the Last Supper, Jesus left them this promise: "I will not leave you as orphans; I will come to you" (John 14:18). Jesus comes to you through the power of his Holy Spirit, whom the Bible calls your comforter and friend. The Holy Spirit leads, guides, and shows you who you are as a child of God. It is through the Holy Spirit that you hear the voice of the Father speaking to you through the words of the Bible. Through the work of the Holy Spirit in your life, you grow in your understanding of who God says you are as his adopted child.

Around the dirty dishes, bread crumbs, and cups of wine scattered across the table of the Last Supper, Jesus promised his disciples, "But when he, the Spirit of truth, comes, he will guide you into all truth" (John 16:13). It is the role of the Holy Spirit to guide you in your understanding of your true spiritual identity in Christ and reveal to you the wonderful heart of your heavenly Father.

> **The Holy Spirit leads, guides, and shows you who you are as a child of God.**

There is no more powerful idea in Scripture than understanding the full implications of the truth that God is for you and who you are as his adopted child. The whole purpose of Christ dying on the cross and rising from the dead was so that you might be adopted into the family of God.

Who Do You Say I Am?

In your head, you may know you're a child of God, but in your heart, you may not always feel like a part of God's family. You struggle enough trying to understand *who* you are let alone *whose* you are. If figuring out your own identity is difficult, understanding your spiritual identity in Christ can seem overwhelming.

You're not alone in figuring this stuff out. For most of the three years Jesus' disciples were with him, they didn't have a clear grasp of who they were as children of

God. The disciples were not a bunch of starched-shirt-smiling-"Kum ba yah"-singing-flannelgraph followers of God. The guys who followed Jesus were a bunch of temperamental-infighting-bullheaded-power-seeking-tail-between-the-legs-misfits whom Jesus chose to change the world. Jesus patiently modeled how to live as a beloved Son of God, but except on rare occasions, the disciples didn't understand who Jesus was. And these were Jesus' best friends!

Jesus was walking with his disciples one day when he surprised them with a pop quiz. Call it an identity question: "Who do people say the Son of Man is?" *Hmm, good question,* the disciples thought, scratching their chins. No one had read the latest Gallup poll, but everyone had a different opinion. Some people thought Jesus was John the Baptist, which made for interesting family ties since John and Jesus were related. Other people thought Jesus was one of the prophets back in action from the dead like Elijah or Jeremiah. The Pharisees called Jesus a blaspheming, demon-possessed Samaritan. Others called him "Rabbi." The woman at the well could see that he was a prophet. And the motorcycle-wheeling paparazzi could never quite get close enough for an accurate photo op of just who Jesus was.

After Jesus heard all of the disciples' feedback, he flipped the question on them: "Who do you say I am?" Never one to be shy, Simon Peter stepped up and responded in his most confident fish-salesman voice, "You are the Christ, the Son of the living God."

Can't you see the smile on Jesus' face? Imagine him thinking to himself, *Peter gets it. He really gets it . . . Peter knows who I am.* Jesus walked up to Peter, looked straight into his eyes, and said, "Blessed are you, Simon son of Jonah, for this was not revealed to you by man, but by my Father in heaven" (Matt. 16:17).

If we are going live as the children of God, we need to muster up the courage to ask God the same thing. "God, who do you say I am?"

Are you willing to ask that question?

I hope so, because God certainly has a lot of great things to say about you. Ultimately, who you really are can only be revealed by your Father in heaven, and it is the amazing, miraculous work of the Holy Spirit that allows your heart to believe the words "This is my son, my daughter, my beloved, whom I love and with whom I'm well pleased." The truth of who you are comes from the truth of God's Word and God working through other Christians to speak his truth into your life. Believing that you are a beloved child of God is evidence of the Holy Spirit at work in your life.

> As a child of God, you are now royalty. A son or daughter of the King of Kings. Through Christ, you are an heir to all the adoptive rights and privileges that come with being a child of God.

With your adoption into the family of God comes a whole new understanding of who God says you are and who you are in Christ. As a child of God, you are now royalty. A son or daughter of the King of Kings. Through Christ, you are an heir to all the adoptive rights and privileges that come with being a child of God (Gal. 4:4–5). What matters most in life is not who others say you are, but who God says you are. Romans 8:31 says, "If God is for us, who can be against us?"

You Are Chosen

The Bible presents a clear, life-transforming message that you have been chosen to know God through his Son, Jesus Christ. God selected the nation of Israel to be his chosen people, and through Jesus the Messiah, all people can become the children of God. Whether your life has been marked by the understanding of being loved and accepted by your family and friends or has been marred by the sting of rejection and the ugliness of self-hatred, the Bible offers a consistent message that you have been chosen by God since the foundation of the world. Linger on God's tender words toward you . . .

> For you are a people holy to the LORD your God. Out of all the peoples on the face of the earth, the LORD has chosen you to be his treasured possession.
>
> Deuteronomy 14:2

> I took you from the ends of the earth,
> from its farthest corners I called you.

I said, "You are my servant";
  I have chosen you and have not rejected you.
So do not fear, for I am with you;
  do not be dismayed, for I am your God.
I will strengthen you and help you;
  I will uphold you with my righteous right hand.

Isaiah 41:9—10

For he chose us in him before the creation of the world to be holy and blameless in his sight. In love he predestined us to be adopted as his sons through Jesus Christ, in accordance with his pleasure and will—to the praise of his glorious grace, which he has freely given us in the One he loves.

Ephesians 1:4—6

But you are a chosen people, a royal priesthood, a holy nation, a people belonging to God, that you may declare the praises of him who called you out of darkness into his wonderful light. Once you were not a people, but now you are the people of God; once you had not received mercy, but now you have received mercy.

1 Peter 2:9—10

God's choosing of you can be summed up in the words of Jesus: "You did not choose me, but I chose you" (John 15:16). Whatever your past, whatever your background, whether you're rich or poor, black or white, Asian or Hispanic, an Ivy League lawyer or a high school dropout, a victim or an overcomer, above all else, God the Father, your Father, chooses YOU! Whatever you've been named and whatever scars you live with, God chooses you because his relentless love can do no other.

Knowing whose you are and knowing that God is for you is the truth that can change your life. Jeremiah 1:5 says, "Before I formed you in the womb, I chose you." Before anyone else named you, God named you "Chosen." Before you experienced any trauma or tragedy or triumph that shaped your identity, God said, "I choose you."

We can run from this truth, but we can never hide. You may feel so beat up, defeated, and discouraged by life that you don't even want to hear that you are chosen by God. If you have a hard time accepting this truth, you need to know that you're not the first who has wrestled with God. If being chosen is enough to make you scream, you might want to sit down for what's next.

You Are the Beloved of God

The Song of Solomon is an entire book dedicated to the passionate love story between God and the people of Israel. If anyone thinks God is a prude, flipping through the eight provocative chapters of the Song of Solomon will leave them and all readers hot and bothered. God, the pursuer of his people, offers an intimate, strong, and tender love for his beloved. In it, he writes, "My beloved is mine, and I am his" (2:16 NASB). In this love story,

Israel the Beloved responds, "I am my beloved's, and his desire is for me" (7:10 NASB).

Have you dared to call yourself the beloved of God? Dared to consider yourself the center of God's desire? Sounds a little audacious, a bit presumptuous, doesn't it? Read Solomon's words and you won't find a hint of presumption. God is deliberate. Intentional. Passionate in his search of you. God loves you with all the obsession and desire of a young lover in pursuit of his beloved. The pages of Scripture are rife with God's wildly lavish love for you. Here's a small slice of what all human hearts long for . . .

> I will give you a new heart and put a new spirit in you; I will remove from you your heart of stone and give you a heart of flesh. And I will put my Spirit in you and move you to follow my decrees and be careful to keep my laws.
>
> Ezekiel 11:19

> How great is the love the Father has lavished on us, that we should be called children of God! And that is what we are! The reason the world does not know us is that it did not know him.
>
> 1 John 3:1

> What, then, shall we say in response to this? If God is for us, who can be against us? He who did not spare his own Son, but gave him up for us all—how will he not also, along with him, graciously give us all things? Who

will bring any charge against those whom God has chosen? It is God who justifies. Who is he that condemns? Christ Jesus, who died—more than that, who was raised to life—is at the right hand of God and is also interceding for us. Who shall separate us from the love of Christ? Shall trouble or hardship or persecution or famine or nakedness or danger or sword? As it is written:

"For your sake we face death all day long;
    we are considered as sheep to be slaughtered."

No, in all these things we are more than conquerors through him who loved us. For I am convinced that neither death nor life, neither angels nor demons, neither the present nor the future, nor any powers, neither height nor depth, nor anything else in all creation, will be able to separate us from the love of God that is in Christ Jesus our Lord.

                                                  Romans 8:31–39

Jesus replied, "If anyone loves me, he will obey my teaching. My Father will love him, and we will come to him and make our home with him."

                                                  John 14:23

A new heart. A new spirit. Lavish love. Inseparable love. Our hearts at home with our Father. No longer living with orphaned hearts. Is it possible to imagine being loved so deeply, so tenderly, so passionately, that nothing, absolutely nothing could sever you from that love? When

73

we do sin, you and I are just one confession away from God. Why? Because we're his children.

The apostle Paul says he's absolutely convinced that nothing can separate him from God's love. Are you convinced? Before God got ahold of his heart, Paul was a Jesus-hating murderer. He stood in the shadows of Stephen's stoning at Jerusalem's Hard Rock Cafe. He found his identity in his power and position as a Pharisee. His spiritual identity was based on his performance, his ethnicity, his pedigree, and his own religious measuring stick. But when Paul's life was changed by the power of God, he experienced an amazing transformation in his spiritual identity. He considered everything as dung or rubbish compared to knowing Christ.

> If anyone else thinks he has reasons to put confidence in the flesh, I have more: circumcised on the eighth day, of the people of Israel, of the tribe of Benjamin, a Hebrew of Hebrews; in regard to the law, a Pharisee; as for zeal, persecuting the church; as for legalistic righteousness, faultless.
>
> But whatever was to my profit I now consider loss for the sake of Christ. What is more, I consider everything a loss compared to the surpassing greatness of knowing Christ Jesus my Lord, for whose sake I have lost all things. I consider them rubbish, that I may gain Christ and be found in him.
>
> Philippians 3:4–9

Despite his sin of being an accomplice to murder and a persecutor of the church, Paul was convinced and confident that he was chosen, loved, and accepted by God. Paul lived with the unquenchable assurance that God was for him. You can live with the same confidence. No matter how tainted your past, God is able and willing to transform you!

What about the woman caught in adultery in John 8? How many men did she sleep with? What was her body count? How many tricks did she turn before she met the one who could see right through her heart? Jesus gave her a new heart and a new spirit . . . what about you? If Jesus stared into the hearts of adulterers and penetrated the minds of murderers, don't you think he could do the same for me and you?

The first voice to listen to when you awake in the morning is that same loving voice that has been calling you all your life. It is the voice of God that says in a simple and tender way, "You are my beloved." This is the most important truth of who you are: You are the beloved of God. By listening for God's voice from the pages of Scripture, you can begin your day with the response of your heart, saying to him, "Yes, God, I am your beloved. Your desire is for me, and my desire is for you."

This is the truth you have to keep coming back to again and again throughout the day. It is the only compass for your heart to find its true north in God. Only when you and I are rooted in being the beloved of God can we know and experience his immeasurable love for us. Henri Nouwen writes,

God runs in passionate pursuit of you, and nothing you do can prevent his relentless hunt for your heart.

When our deepest truth is that we are the Beloved and when our greatest joy and peace come from fully claiming that truth, it follows that this has to become visible and tangible in the ways we eat and drink, talk and love, play and work. When the deepest currents of our life no longer have any influence on the waves at the surface, then our vitality will eventually ebb, and we will end up listless and bored even when we are busy.[6]

God's Word affirms that you are his beloved and he is the lover of your soul. God runs in passionate pursuit of you, and nothing you do can prevent his relentless hunt for your heart. Jesus is the beloved Son of God, and if you walk with him each day, his Spirit will show you how to become the beloved son or daughter you are meant to be.

You Are Accepted

Yeah, but . . . does God really accept me? Does he really accept me for who I am? You don't know my story. No, I don't. But God does.

We all have our "yeah, buts." But with God, there are no ifs, ands, or buts about it. In Christ, God accepts you and adopts you into his family. What's at stake here is not your good name or reputation but God's good name. "For the sake of his great name the LORD will not reject his people, because the LORD was pleased to make you his own" (1 Sam. 12:22). If it pleases God to make us his children, isn't it enough for us to say, "Well, okay, if you say so . . ."

If there is anyone who understands rejection and, specifically, understands *your* rejection, it is Jesus. You may have suffered rejection by a workaholic father or a mother too consumed by her own problems. In school, you may have been tagged the geek, the fatso, the brain, the slut, the loner, or just a loser. Were you rejected by a broken marriage engagement? Rejected by a husband or wife? Rejected by your in-laws so that nothing you do will ever earn their favor? Rejected your employers and lost a job promotion? Or what about the heartbreaking rejection that comes from being estranged from a son or daughter who wants nothing to do with you?

Rejection transmogrifies itself into all sorts of hideous shapes and sizes, but at the crossroads of rejection is Jesus, your Savior and friend who understands your rejection like no one else in this world.

Long before Christ was born, Isaiah prophesied that Jesus would suffer all the rejection this world could dish out. Isaiah writes, "He was despised and rejected by men, a man of sorrows, and familiar with suffering" (Isa. 53:3). Jesus squared off against the Pharisees' rejection of his work: "I have come in my Father's name, and you do not accept me; but if someone else comes in his own name, you will accept him" (John 5:43). Predicting his own death, Jesus revealed to his disciples that "the Son of Man must suffer many things and be rejected by the elders, chief priests and teachers of the law, and that he must be killed and after three days rise again" (Mark 8:31).

In accepting the rejection of this world by dying on the cross, Jesus became the one and only acceptable sacrifice for sin so that we could experience the full acceptance of God as his children. Paul writes, "Very rarely will anyone die for a righteous man, though for a good man someone might possibly dare to die. But God demonstrates his own love for us in this: While we were still sinners, Christ died for us" (Rom. 5:7–8).

God's relentless love for you is not mere words or a Hallmark greeting card of sappy spiritual sentiments. God proves he is for you by deliberate action, clearly demonstrating his love for you by allowing his Son to suffer brutal rejection so that you could experience the awesome, overwhelming power of his acceptance.

As a dad, I cannot describe in words how much I love my kids, but my love for my kids pales in comparison to how much God loves all of his children. If you have children, the depth of how much you love children is but an inkling of the love and grace God has for you.

My daughter Ellie has a very specific bedtime ritual. She neatly arranges four or five of her favorite stuffed animals close to her. Then she draws her thick down comforter tightly around her neck so that the only thing peeking out from underneath the covers is her little face. We say our prayers, and then she asks for her daily hug, which is not the only hug of the day but the last one, which makes it her daily hug. Sometimes I'll softly brush my fingers across her forehead as the rising moon casts its gray glow against her face. In a soft whisper, I'll say to her, "Who are you to me?"

Ellie knows the answer. "I'm your beloved."

"That's right, sweetheart . . . you're my beloved."

My heart's desire is that my children will grow up knowing that they are the beloved of God because they have experienced my wholehearted love, affection, and acceptance. I don't always get it right as a dad, but by allowing my heart to be beloved of God, I have a great and wonderful gift to give away. By accepting and resting in the truth that God is for me, I have a very simple truth to share with others.

I hope by now that the truth that you are a chosen, loved, and accepted child of God is beginning to penetrate the deepest caverns of your heart. But be on your guard. There is someone who wants to unravel all the good and perfect things God is doing in your life. God is for us, but the Bible is very clear that there is someone who is against us. You have a spiritual enemy who wants to mess with your adoption papers and would love to throw you back into the orphanage. For every word of love spoken to you by God, there is another voice. Another whisper from the wilderness trying to woo you away from the love of God.

FIVE

Three Whispers from the Wilderness

My mom recently called me to come over to the house and pick up "my box." As one of seven kids from a large Irish Catholic family, here I was in my late thirties, and my parents were still picking up after me. Though I had left home long ago, I had forgotten about some of the things I'd left behind. I didn't even remember there was a box with my name on it.

I drove over to my folks' home, greeted my mom with a hug, and followed her into the garage, where she led me to a cardboard fruit box sitting on the floor. Inside, the box was filled with stuff I hadn't seen in a long time. I began to dig inside its contents. Recollections, some fond and a few painful, seemed to jump out at me. Each held fingerprints from my past. Memories I had not touched in years.

When I was young, my mom had saved a few choice creations I had made in school, and here they were in my box. I pulled out a kindergarten paper plate crèche with my picture on it. There was a swatch of pink burlap with a bunny pattern stitched into it with red yarn. I remembered making that in first grade. Other notable artwork, destined, I'm sure, for European museums when I'm dead and gone, like my finger-paint designs and other assorted artwork, were stacked in the box. I dug through elementary school class pictures and old report cards. I found a first communion photo of me wearing a white shirt and blue tie. Letters from old eighth grade girlfriends—how those got saved, I have no clue. A high school annual or two. There were postcards from when I was traveling overseas in college and old prom pictures. Scary.

Rummaging around, I dug deeper in the box. Buried underneath some old report cards was something round and hard. I pulled it out of the box, and before me was an old baseball glued to a thick block of lacquered brown wood. Signed in thick red ink, the ball read "Phillies '73." It was my Phillies team trophy. The coach had given one to each boy as an award just for getting out, playing hard, and being part of a team. Winning didn't really matter. Being a part of something larger than ourselves did.

The ball had been signed in red ink by all my teammates. I hadn't seen the ball in years, but in a split second, my memory went to the movies, and I was back playing first base. I could smell the fresh-cut grass. My teammates were screaming at the batter, challenging his nine-year-old manhood, daring him to swing against our pitcher. All we wanted was our turn at bat. That's why boys play baseball. As we stand at home plate, all we want to do is slug the ball as hard as we can. A hit gets us on base, of course, but ask any man who's ever played Little League, and he'll tell you that what every boy really dreams of is slugging the ball into the stratosphere.

I looked at the pile of stuff in my box. Years and years of accumulated memories. So many events, experiences, thoughts, dreams, longings, successes, defeats, fears, and losses were tied to that box. That box represented my life up until age twenty-three, which is when, sometime after college, I stopped dumping things into it.

By then, my identity was pretty well formed. So I thought. Our twenties are when we stop filling our box with the things of childhood and begin a new search to fill our box with the stuff of adulthood. Our identity gets tied to new things. In different seasons of our life, we fill our box with all those things we think are necessary to create an identity. Much of our box-filling work is subconscious, and most of us are not even aware of our reasons or motives for what we put in our box.

Adulthood is all about rummaging through our box and understanding our identity, whose we really are, so that we might have a clear vision to accurately help our spouses, children, friends, and co-workers see whose they are. If you and I understand that we are the chosen, loved, and accepted children of God made in his image, then we can reflect the same chosenness, love, and acceptance to those we live with and encounter each day. Nothing is more important than receiving the gift of your chosenness, so that you might give to others the gift of their chosenness.

To develop a spiritual identity as a child of God, you must know what's in your box and how it got there. But what you may not realize is that someone has a scheme and strategy for filling your box with a false identity you were never meant to have. If you're not aware of his whispers, you just might end up creating your own identity that will ultimately box you in. Your spiritual enemy loves to entice you with plenty of options and opportunities. He does not want your identity to be created and centered in whose you are as a child of God. Satan stands waiting, whispering from the wilderness, and his scheme for you is the exact same strategy he tried on Jesus.

> Nothing is more important than receiving the gift of your chosenness from God by becoming his beloved, so that you might give to others the gift of their chosenness.

Whispers from the Wilderness

If you feel like you're the only one who hears whispers calling you to fill your box with things you know will never satisfy you, then you are not alone. You are not the first to hear whispers in the wilderness. As I flip through the pages of Scripture, the Bible confirms that every temptation, every difficulty, every problem, predicament, or dilemma that you and I experience is something Jesus went through himself. When Jesus spent forty days in the wilderness, Satan tried to fill Jesus' box with everything and anything that would sever his relationship with his Father.

If you feel discouraged by your lack of spiritual progress, overwhelmed by life's burdens, or simply beat up by others trying to squeeze you into their mold, you can take great encouragement in knowing that Jesus understands the temptations you're going through. God knows his children get tempted and tested. Because Jesus understands what's going on in your heart, you can come to him, weaknesses and all, with confidence.

For we do not have a high priest who is unable to sympathize with our weaknesses, but we have one who has been tempted in every way, just as we are—yet was without sin. Let us then approach the throne of grace with confidence, so that we may receive mercy and find grace to help us in our time of need.

Hebrews 4:15–16

Immediately after his baptism, when Jesus is named by his Father, the Holy Spirit sends Jesus out into the desert. Jesus spends the next forty days and nights going mano a mano with Satan. In the wilderness, he hears dark whispers tempting him to drown out the familiar voice of his Father and to forge a sense of identity apart from God. The wilderness is the proving ground where Jesus declares whose he really is. In the vast sea of rock, sand, and scrub brush, Satan attempts to undo who Jesus is as the chosen, loved, and accepted Son of God. Everything Satan says and does is an assault on Jesus' identity and God's purpose for his life and his plan of redemption.

The same garbage Satan pulls on Jesus is the same trash-talking stuff he pulls on us. Let's take a look at the three specific whispers from the wilderness Satan used to attack Jesus' identity as the Son of God.

Whisper #1: Provide for Yourself

Alone. Sunburned. Dehydrated. Dying for a Subway sandwich and a fifty-gallon drum of Gatorade, Jesus has been fasting for forty days and his stomach is screaming. He is at his weakest point when up strolls his mortal enemy. "The tempter came to him and said, 'If you are the Son of God, tell these stones to become bread'" (Matt. 4:3). In this first ploy, Satan seems to take the most obvious path of least resistance: Jesus' appetite. Satan knows the way to a man's heart is through his stomach, and Jesus hasn't had a hot bagel in weeks. Bread appears to be the main issue here, right?

There's no question that Jesus is hungry. If he wants to pull out a rotisserie for roasting a few desert rocks, he could, but fresh-baked bread is not at the heart of this temptation. Bread is simply the tool Satan is trying to use to manipulate Jesus into denying a greater reality. The operative word here is *if*. Satan is attacking Jesus' identity and who he is as the Son of God. Jesus, *if* you're really the Son of God, *if* you're really who you say you are, make your own manna. Jesus, *if* you're really the Son of God, provide for yourself. Jesus, *if* you're really the chosen one, you don't need your dad to make you a sandwich, do you?

For the past forty days, Jesus has been absolutely dependent on his heavenly Father. Satan wants to move Jesus' heart from a place of total dependence on God to a state of self-sufficient independence. He wants Jesus to prove who he is by providing for himself. What's at stake here is not a sandwich but Jesus' understanding of who he is as the Son of God. Is Jesus' identity based on the truth that his Father promises to meet his deepest and every need? Or is his identity founded on the lie that he doesn't need God because he can handle things on his own?

Sound familiar? How much of your life is spent depending on no one but yourself to get your needs met? How have you gained your sense of identity by your ability to take matters into your own hands and control the desired outcome? When you were a child, what experiences taught you that your emotional, physical, relational, and spiritual needs were not important? When did your heart learn that it is better to go it alone than to trust others? How have you been duped into believing "*If* you're really somebody, make your mark on this world by providing for yourself"?

Independence is a highly touted value in our society, but is your view of yourself shaped by self-sufficient independence or absolute dependence as a child of God who trusts your heavenly Father to meet your every need?

> When you were a child, what experiences taught you that your emotional, physical, relational, and spiritual needs were not important? When did your heart learn that it is better to go it alone than to trust others?

What was Jesus' response? He tells Satan where his true nourishment comes from. "Man does not live on bread alone, but on every word that comes from the mouth of God" (Matt. 4:4). Did you get that . . . every word that comes from the mouth of God. What words did Jesus hear forty days earlier?

"This is my Son, my beloved, whom I love and in whom I'm well pleased."

To know whose you are, you have to choose who you are going to listen to. Jesus can choose to listen to who his Father already says he is as a chosen, loved, and accepted Son. Or he can listen to Satan's whisper and the seeds of doubt by accepting the challenge to provide for himself. If Satan can get Jesus to take matters into his own hands by proving his independence apart from his Father, he can have another slave who doesn't want the privilege of being a son. Remember, Jesus is hungry, but he is not starving. His satisfaction and sense of self, what really fills and feeds him, is based on whose he is as a Son.

Are you tempted to provide for yourself? To live life independent from God? Call it an identity attack. Someone is leading you away from the voice of your Father. Someone is trying to get you to identify with what you can do instead of what God can do.

Maybe you came from deprivation and poverty. Have you vowed to never put yourself in the same economic position as your father and mother? Do you hear whispers from the wilderness calling you to pull yourself up by your own bootstraps? To trust in no one but yourself? There's nothing wrong with industriousness, ambition, and setting goals, but if you are not aware of the core forces that drive you, you will fall into the overwhelmingly strong temptation to wrap your identity around your ability to provide for yourself.

Your heavenly Father knows and wants to meet your needs. Scripture is filled with wonderful promises of God's provision for you. And one of the marks of being a child is trusting your Father to meet your needs. It is also a sign of being Jesus' disciple. In the Sermon on the Mount, Jesus said,

So do not worry, saying, "What shall we eat?" or "What shall we drink?" or "What shall we wear?" For the pagans run after all these things, and your heavenly Father knows that you need them. But seek first his kingdom and his righteousness, and all these things will be given to you as well.

Matthew 6:31–33

In Christ, we are loved children of God. Because we are children of God, we don't have to live with the iron fist of control. Your control . . . my control . . . is an illusion. We don't have to try to control others, our circumstances, or our own life. We can, instead, live in the freedom that comes with trusting our Father who is in complete control. You and I are most free when we let go of our control by abandoning ourselves to what our heavenly Father wants. There's no need for us to go it alone. By seeking first our Father's kingdom, we will receive what we need when we need it.

Whisper #2: Prove Yourself

Tom joined my grief recovery class after his father died. When Tom was growing up, his father was an Air Force colonel who treated Tom and his sister as if they were new recruits in boot camp. Nothing Tom did was good enough. He'd score a winning run in a baseball game, and his dad would grill him about why he struck out in the fifth. Every couple years, the family would move across the country, as the military transferred Tom's father from base to base. Tom lived between the extremes of his father's absence and a strict military code. Before his father died, Tom longed to hear his father say that he loved him. But those words never came. Tom's dad went to the grave with what Tom needed most.

Now a successful business executive and owner of his own company, Tom found that his achievements and prosperity didn't bring him the satisfaction he thought they would. All the money in the world could never purchase the love of his father. For years, ever since he was a boy, Tom sought his father's approval. Baseball trophies. Straight As. Nothing Tom did was ever good enough. Tom had a gifted mind and sharp entrepreneurial skills, but without his father's love, he still had a hole in his heart.

The very hole Satan wants to exploit.

The very identity longing Satan wants to assault.

If Satan can't get Jesus to provide for himself, maybe, just maybe, he might get him to scratch that identity itch by proving who he really is. If Jesus could just prove who he really is, then that would settle the question of who he is once and for all, right?

Then the devil took him to the holy city and had him stand on the highest point of the temple. "If you are the Son of God," he said, "throw yourself down. For it is written:

" 'He will command his angels concerning you,
  and they will lift you up in their hands,
so that you will not strike your foot against a stone.' "

Matthew 4:5–6

How much of your identity is tied to your performance?

Satan isn't very creative. He's using that *if* word again. Hey, Jesus, *if* you're the Son of God, why not show everyone a swan dive from the top of the temple? *If* you're the Son of God, prove to the rest of Jerusalem how many angels you have for personal assistants. *If* you're really who you say you are, prove it. Prove it by your power. Prove it by your performance. Prove it by having God protect you. Just prove it.

Jesus ain't taking the bait. He knows whose he is, so he has nothing to prove.

Satan is tempting Jesus to throw himself down from the temple, the center of worship for the nation of Israel, but Jesus throws it back in his face. "It is also written: 'Do not put the Lord your God to the test'" (Matt. 4:7).

How much of your identity is tied to your performance? Your accomplishments and achievements? Your trophies and awards? Your sales goals? How organized you are or how clean your house is? How tethered are you to the opinions of others? Do you crumble when someone offers you constructive criticism and perceive it as an attack? How much of your identity is tied to seeking the approval of a mother or father who never said they loved you? A mother or father who offered you a pay-for-performance standard of loving? How many of your days are spent proving that you are worthy of someone else's love? Proving to yourself and others that you are worthy of being chosen, loved, and accepted?

For the first ten years of my life, I grew up in the same neighborhood and had many experiences of being loved and accepted just for who I was. I had all my buddies, friends I'd grown up with since kindergarten. It wasn't until I moved from Los Angeles to Dana Point that I experienced loneliness for the first time. Our first and only family move began a process of me going to six different schools in six years. Before, I didn't have to prove myself to anyone, but as I jumped from school to school, I now had to prove myself worthy of others' friendship. And so I became a performer.

For me, the story that crystallizes my search for acceptance begins with catching a football. It was the first week at my new school in Laguna Beach, and I had spent more than a few days eating lunch by myself. A bunch of the other sixth grade guys were starting a game of football, and they were short one player. So they asked me, the new kid. Eager to fit in, I said yes, and everyone got set for the kickoff.

The opposing team kicked off. The ball sailed in the air and drifted in my direction. I caught it, and to my surprise, I ran it all the way down the field for a touchdown. That was my ticket. Performing, for the most part, has been my ticket to belonging, and I have been catching footballs ever since.

Though my junior high football touchdown never led to an NFL career, I can look back over the past forty years of my life and honestly say that I have received most of my approval, strokes, and attention because of my performance. It's what has worked for me to earn love and praise. It wasn't until my thirties that I began to realize that my identity was based too much on performance instead of on simply resting in being a child of God. The past ten years have been a slow and difficult process of learning that I don't have to prove myself or perform for God to win his love.

As boys and girls, we are wired to please our parents, and we want to hear those one or two voices cheering us on. I was fortunate to grow up in a home in which the parents were great cheerleaders. But even so, who doesn't spend their early years proving, in one way or another, that they are worthy of love? We all long for unconditional love and acceptance.

Whatever uniform you wore as a child, you still felt the same need and the longing for approval. You might have been a five-year-old little girl dressed as a ballerina. Or a seven-year-old at a piano recital. A nine-year-old boy playing baseball. A ten-year-old girl playing soccer. A middle school girl getting dressed for her first dance. A freshman football player. Let your heart wander back to when you were growing up. Where were you? What were you wearing? Most important, who was there watching you? What did they say? What didn't they say? What were you seeking?

We weren't just hitting or playing or performing to win the competition . . . we were performing to win the heart of our father or mother. We wanted to be seen. We wanted to be noticed. We were doing our best just so we could hear those few choice words, "Well done. Great job. I knew you could do it." And when we flubbed our line in the school play or missed the shot at the buzzer, what we really needed was encouragement and not a harsh repri-mand. We hoped that our parents' love wasn't dependent on our performance, the goals we made, the grades we achieved, or the trophies we earned. All we wanted to hear, in one way or another, was that we were loved just for being a son or a daughter. And that was good enough. Is your heart still longing to hear those words?

Whisper #3: Pleasure Yourself

If Satan can't get you to fall for the temptation of self-sufficiency or the temptation of proving that you are worthy of other people's love, the last card he will play is the one card, the one illusion, that catches everyone's eye: *You can have it all*.

Again, the devil took him to a very high mountain and showed him all the kingdoms of the world and their splendor. "All this I will give you," he said, "if you will bow down and worship me."

95

Jesus said to him, "Away from me, Satan! For it is written: 'Worship the Lord your God, and serve him only.'"

Then the devil left him, and angels came and attended him.

Matthew 4:8–11

Notice the change in Satan's strategy. He can't get Jesus to prove that he is the Son of God. Jesus already knows whose he is, and he ain't budging. Showing his absolute dependence on his heavenly Father, Jesus refuses to provide for himself or perform for Satan. Okay, Jesus, name your price. Everyone's got a price. So Satan takes Jesus to a high mountain, and in a flash, every kingdom and every comforting pleasure is displayed before his eyes. Wine. Women. Riches. A George Foreman grill and a new car! Satan plays a combo game of *The Price Is Right* and *Wheel of Fortune* with one condition: All this I will give you, if you will bow down and worship me.

And we take the bait. How many of us have bought the pleasure-seeking lie that we can have it all? We deserve it all? We need it all? Satan whispers in the wilderness of our most hidden hurts that all of our deepest needs, our heart's strongest longings, will be met in proving, performing, providing, and pleasuring ourselves. Daily we hear the whispers: *Do this and all the world will be yours. You'll be happy. You deserve it. You're entitled to a better life. You've worked hard for it. You owe it to yourself. You're not getting what you deserve.* And the greatest lie of all: *You're all alone . . . it all depends on you.*

So instead of seeking to find our identity in being the chosen, loved, and accepted children of God, we run off in search of other lovers who promise us pleasure but leave us with a hollow sense of nothingness and the question "Is this all I have to live for?" Unaware of Satan's schemes to steal, kill, and destroy, we literally buy into a warped sense of identity by attaching our sense of self to stuff. We reject who God already says we are. Fortunately, we have a Savior "who has been tempted in every way, just as we are—yet was without sin" (Heb. 4:15). In this third and final assault on his identity, Jesus issues the command, "Away from me, Satan! For it is written: 'Worship the Lord your God, and serve him only'" (Matt. 4:10).

Jesus shows us whose he really is, and it is all a matter of worship. We give our lives to what we worship. Worship is at the heart of every temptation, because we will become like whatever we worship. We worship movie stars and professional athletes. We worship our "teams" even though they may be last place in the NFL or NBA. We worship our cars. Our stock portfolios. The equity in our homes. Our comforts and lifestyles. Our bodies. Anything we attach our identity to is what we worship.

As I flip through a local Orange County magazine, I see so many ads for plastic surgery and every imaginable "enhancement" for our bodies. I wonder if there are more plastic surgeons in Orange County than houses of worship? Look inside your check register, and there you'll see your priorities and what you worship. Aside from basic life necessities, we really don't need very much. All the rest is filler, and it is Satan's goal for us to fill our boxes with everything but God. Whom or what we worship defines who we really are. What we worship defines whom we will serve.

> Our character is shaped by the things we worship. People who worship money become greedy. Those who worship power become ruthless. Men who worship women become lustful. People who worship themselves become arrogant. But those who worship the true and living God become Christ-like.[7]

Jesus defines who he is as the Son of God by refusing to bow down to Satan's seductive schemes. His sole desire is to serve his Father. Because he knows his Father is well pleased with him, Jesus wants to please his Father. Nothing else will satisfy. Nothing else comes close.

Whom or what we worship defines who we really are. What we worship defines whom we will serve.

The "three *P*s." Provide for yourself. Prove yourself. Pleasure yourself. These are the three whispers from the wilderness. Satan's hat trick of temptation was an all-out assault on the identity of Jesus. Satan's strategy was to isolate Jesus from his Father. And his plan for us is no different. If we stay spiritually isolated from our Father and ourselves, we will forever pursue a false sense of self made up of outer appearances, while we live wholly unaware of whose we really are.

My Phillies baseball trophy now sits on the desk where I write. It came from my box. You have your own box, with your own memories and stories. In it are all the voices you heard with your ears and now hold in your heart. Yet still, you hope that there's more to your life than what is in your box. And there is. As we rummage through our memories, searching for old photos, digging for glimpses of love, listening for the truth of whose we are, there is another Voice: You don't have to provide for yourself. You don't have to prove yourself worthy of love. And you don't have to pursue a life of pleasure to find meaning and significance. You don't have to earn what you already have. In the midst of our wondering and waiting, our heavenly Father already has given us the answer:

You are my child, whom I love, my beloved, in whom I'm well pleased.

Even when you feel disfigured, unloved, and lost in a wilderness filled with enticing whispers, there is always that one Voice that speaks through the brokenness. God desires to lead you out of the wilderness, but for some of us, the path of brokenness is the only way to get there.

SIX

Broken Wholeness

On the walls of my office, I have several colorful mosaic crosses of different shapes and sizes. The largest is a three-and-a-half-foot Celtic cross made of plywood; broken travertine tiles surround the inner and outer four points of the cross, circled by a vibrant ring of broken blue, white, green, black, and burnt sienna colored tiles. My Celtic cross is so heavy, if it ever came down on someone, it'd be like dropping a pallet of tile on their head.

Other crosses on my wall are smaller, made of broken dinner plates or stained glass. Over the past couple years, I've given away many as presents or auction items for charity raffles, but I never imagined the day when people would pop into my office offering to pay cash for one. Though something inside of me resists the idea of selling my mosaics, when someone walks in my office and subtly hints that they would love to have one, I do receive a lot of joy by pulling one off the wall and surprising them with the words, "You like it . . . it's yours."

I affectionately call the crosses my "art therapy," but there is more truth to that statement than not. I began making mosaics about four years ago in the midst of a very painful season of personal brokenness. I have lived with chronic pain for the past eleven years, and four years ago I hit a physical and emotional wall by entering a dark cavern of depression like nothing I'd ever experienced before. I felt like the broken mosaic of a shattered windshield, my life splintered into a zillion tiny pieces as I tried to keep pace with everything going on around me. Every day was a strange, almost surreal experience, as I begged God for help and strength.

For the previous seven years, I had lived with chronic pain from acute tendonitis in both wrists as a result of sitting at a keyboard for five or six hours a day. The wrist pain initially began three weeks after I lost my youth ministry job at a church where I'd worked for seven years. At the time, I was thirty years old. We had just had our second baby, and I had no idea what my future held. So I typed away like a madman.

The pain intensity varied from day to day. On some days, it was low to moderate. Many days, the pain was intense.

As I sat at the keyboard, I felt like someone was pushing pins in my wrists, dousing them with gasoline, and then *whoosh*, lighting the whole mess into a finger-burning wrist flambé. Ask anyone who has lived with chronic pain and you will find no shortage of stories. I did anything I could to get out of the pain. Cortisone shots. Acupuncture. Advil for breakfast, lunch, and dinner. Physical therapy ad infinitum. Ergonomic computer gadgets. Chiropractors. Massage. Special herbs, vitamins, and nasty drinks that tasted like used car oil. A wild alternative therapy called "prolotherapy" that blessed me with ninety full-gauge needle shots in each arm! Wheat-free, sugar-free, caffeine-free diets. Colon cleansing. I'll stop now. My attempts to cure my inflamed wrists could fill volumes of medical journals.

I know, I told myself one day, *I'll use voice-activated computer software. Instead of typing into a computer, I'll just speak into a computer.* After talking like a robot into a computer for a year, I wore out my vocal cords and lost my voice for five months. What you need, my friends told me, is a wire from your brain into your computer. You're a mess!

After I had lived through seven years of chronic pain, my wheels finally came off in the spring of 2000. I was under a lot of pressure waiting for a multibook deal to come through from another publisher. I was still having chronic problems with my voice. I wasn't sleeping at night. Then, the proverbial straw that broke my back was a weekend of pool play with the kids in Palm Desert.

For the next eight days, I was laid out flat on my back, ushering in a two-and-a-half-month fog of depression. I had no idea chronic pain could so totally wipe a person out. I couldn't work. Couldn't sleep or eat. I lost fourteen pounds. I felt like someone had wrapped my head in three feet of gauze bandages. I was in so much pain I wanted to die. I had no idea that there is a very specific cycle to how chronic pain works, or what it takes to break the cycle. It wasn't until I read the cover story on chronic pain in an issue of the *U.S. News & World Report* that I realized the only way out of my depression was a series of very specific steps to stop the downward, debilitating cycle of pain.

Like never before, my heart felt the darkness and despair described by Jeremiah, the Old Testament prophet, in Lamentations 3. If you have suffered with the brokenness of chronic physical or emotional pain, wondering where God is in the midst of it all, Jeremiah's groanings will sound achingly familiar. When I first read these words, they resonated with what was going on in my heart. Jeremiah speaks of walking in darkness, his flesh growing old, of being walled in and weighed down with chains, surrounded by bitterness and hardship, his prayer shut out from God who lays in wait to pounce and mangle him like a lion, his teeth broken with gravel, trampled in the dust. Small wonder Jeremiah is named the "weeping prophet."

My journey into chronic pain and the resulting depression that unraveled me in the summer of 2000 brought me to a place of utter dependence on God and, eventually, a whole new understanding of who I am as his child. From that experience came the initial seeds of this book. Hitting my lowest forced me to evaluate how much of my identity was tied to my writing and speaking career. What I discovered was that God loved me just for who I was. He didn't love me any more or any less for being a writer or speaker. He loved me just for being his child. A son. Even though my identity was so tightly wrapped around my writing career and making it on my own that it took years of chronic pain and depression to finally cause me to let go.

And so I did. I took a year and a half off from writing. I crawled back into ministry, back to working with people instead of being holed up in my home office, wondering how in the world God could use someone like me in the pathetic mess I was in. But even in my brokenness, I could still see that God had a sense of humor. I returned to work at the same church that had let me go seven years earlier. I now write my books with a pen in each hand, hunting and pecking because it eases the strain on my wrists. For someone who knows how to type fast, this is a very slow way to write a book.

> When I could see absolutely no purpose in my brokenness, God used this to bring me to a new place of wholeness.

And it was during my slow crawl out of depression that I began making mosaics. All that was broken in my life began to take shape into something beautiful God wanted to use for his purpose. When I could see absolutely no purpose in my brokenness, God used this to bring me to a new place of wholeness. For me, my journey into chronic pain has been about identity—spiritual identity.

Yet over the past ten years, though the pain has been overwhelming at times, I have learned that I am not my pain. Pain and suffering is neither the whole of my life story nor the whole of me as a child of God. Chronic pain has been my harshest taskmaster, but when I slow down and get really quiet, it has also been my most gentle instructor. In my brokenness, God has far more access to my heart than he used to. It reminds me that I'm not finished. I still have a long way to go. Pain has taught me how to surrender. There have been many days when I've cried out to God, "Okay! Uncle! Uncle! Uncle five hundred times!" Pain has taught me more about who I am as God's child and life and struggle and perseverance and hope than all the blessings I've ever received. And it still hurts.

Don't Break Anything

Last year, I was asked to lead a mosaic cross project called Worship Factor for the children's arts program at our church. After tracing a large, eight-foot cross on a sheet of plywood, the kids got to cut it out with a jigsaw. Their favorite part of the project, though, was what came next. After gathering around me twenty or so kids holding hammers, I told them, "You have grown up being told not to break things. You are not allowed to break your mom's fine china, your brother's toys, or your sister's stuff. Today, in this class, you get to break as much tile as you want." A roar of enthusiasm went up as the kids dove into the tile boxes. They laughed and screamed as they smashed the tiles, the high shattering noise piercing the air at the moment of impact.

How often are we given permission to break things, let alone given permission to be broken? You and I need permission to be broken. To have seasons in our life when we don't have it all together, just like in winter when the trees are barren of leaves. To have periods in which it's okay to struggle, because out of the struggle something new can emerge. To search for the wholeness that can come out of brokenness. To know it's okay to have a bad day. Or week. Or month. Or year. To not have all the right answers or be able to explain why God is doing what he's doing. To be broken simply because brokenness is part of the human condition.

But people get uneasy if your brokenness hangs around longer than a bad day. People don't know what to do when the wheels fall off your life. They still know the old you, the "you" before you were broken. They don't know the new broken you and neither do you, because you're numb just looking at all the broken shards of your life scattered at your feet.

Think about it: If you've recently had a loved one die—a husband, a wife, a child, a mom or dad—you and your family members will receive a lot of comfort and attention in the first couple weeks following the death. But what happens after three or four weeks? The meals stop. The phone calls stop. No more notes in the mail. People don't mention your loved one's name out of fear that you'll lose it. Four to six weeks after the death, everyone else has been fully engaged in life for weeks. The expectation is for you to do the same. Time to get on with your life. But grief—brokenness—doesn't work like that. Grief isn't a time clock that punches in and out.

> People get uneasy if your brokenness hangs around longer than a bad day. People don't know what to do when the wheels fall off your life.

We all seem to have an independent strain of John Wayne DNA. We don't want to be broken. We want to be bulletproof. We don't want to be weak. We are a society of winners. We don't want to be vulnerable. We want to appear invincible. We don't want to be comforted. We want to be in control. We'd rather pretend than admit we're powerless. We are afraid to admit when we feel worried, anxious, and overwhelmed, so instead we wear a thin veil of superficiality and shallowness. We hide because we're afraid that if we truly open the lid of our hearts to show another person all of our fears and grief and pain, they'd say, "Yuck!" leaving us with deeper feelings of rejection and isolation.

We need permission to be broken. In our society and even in the church, we have erected elaborate defenses against vulnerability, weakness, and suffering to protect our hearts from further disappointment and loss. Our view of the victorious Christian life is more like a caricature of a bulletproof Superman believer who is always strong, never doubting, always smiling, never struggling, and able to leap tall churches in a single bound. We want strong Christians, not puny, weak ones who get sand kicked in their faces.

There's nothing wrong with great strength. Strength alone, though, is not an accurate picture of the whole Christian life. A lot of people don't understand that brokenness is an essential part of being a Christian. Read the stories of the great saints and leaders throughout church history. These are men and women who suffered tremendously but found God's grace absolutely sufficient in every way. And through their suffering, God created something beautiful.

We have a whole theology based on sin, brokenness, redemption, and wholeness, but in our misunderstanding, naiveté, or plain insensitivity, we say the stupidest things when people are hurting. A friend gets cancer or an incurable disease, and we hear someone spout it is because there is sin in his life. An alcoholic relapses, and we point the finger of shame instead of serving a cup of truth and grace. A child's mom dies, and we tell her to be happy that her mom is in heaven. A couple goes through a devastating divorce, and we spout off that God hates divorce, which he does, but have we forgotten that it is our own brokenness that leads us to judge, criticize, and condemn others?

By not knowing what to do with our brokenness or the brokenness of others, we miss hearing the voice of our Father calling out to us. When you're going through a rough time, how often do you hear the popular euphemism, "Oh, don't worry, God won't give you more than you can handle." Really? Show me where that verse appears in the Bible. In this fallen world in which we live, God allows far more than we can handle to show us our true need for him. Brokenness brings us to the end of ourselves. It is the very thing that brings us to our knees. It is the very thing we need to lead us to the wholeness found in Christ. God is not an almighty Advil for pain and affliction. He offers us more than relief, rest, and restoration in the midst of our pain. He offers us his presence. As long as we are strong, independent, self-reliant, and self-sufficient, we will continue to depend on our own devices, ingenuity, skill, resourcefulness, and spiritual entrepreneurship to work out our salvation. We would rather save ourselves than appear weak and needy by depending on God. We give help. We don't ask for it.

This is not how children think or operate. When a child falls and gets hurt, the most natural thing for him to do is run to his mother or father. In Luke 18, Jesus even rebukes his disciples for keeping the kids away: "Let the little children come to me, and do not hinder them, for the kingdom of God belongs to such as these. I tell you the truth, anyone who will not receive the kingdom of God like a little child will never enter it" (vv. 16–17).

Isn't it interesting that Jesus said receiving the kingdom of God like a little child is the condition for entering it? Our brokenness has an uncanny way of sifting through our priorities by causing us to evaluate what matters most in life. Jesus asks us as children of God to bring everything we are, brokenness and all, to him.

Broken Perspectives

The view from Kandee's window was absolutely beautiful. Below her were the wide blue expanse of the Pacific Ocean and the white foam of waves crashing on the barnacle-covered rocks. If she had been staying in the Laguna Beach Montage or Ritz Carlton in Dana Point, a room like this would cost hundreds of dollars a night. But Kandee lay in her bed, the quiet sucking sound of a chemotherapy machine pumping medicine throughout her system. I was sure this was a view most people could do without.

I had just left Michael, another friend of mine battling cancer, at his home in Newport Beach. Visiting two cancer patients in one afternoon made for a sober-

Jesus asks us as children of God to bring everything we are, brokenness and all, to him.

ing day. By the time I returned home, I was in a pensive, reflective mood. I was grateful for my health, wrist pain and all. Grateful that I didn't have a hospital room with a view. Both Michael and Kandee have been tremendous examples to me of courage and resilience in the midst of brokenness and suffering. Their gift to me that day was something I often lose sight of: perspective. Then things got weird.

It was Aidan's birthday, and he was dying to go to Chuck E. Cheese. Krista hates the place for all of its noise and sensory overload, but I'm always up for free game tokens with pizza. As we got out of the car and walked up to the entrance of Chuck E. Cheese, I bumped into a guy I know from church. Call him Don. A couple weeks earlier, Don had walked away from his marriage and two kids. And now here he was at Chuck E. Cheese with his two kids and new girlfriend. Hiding behind a mask of drug use, credit card debt, and who knows what other secrets, Don left his wife under the guise that his personal needs were not being met in the marriage.

Don introduced his girlfriend to me as if she were his sister. We exchanged pleasantries. And an icy shiver went down my back. An awkward encounter, to say the least. My mind flashed back to Kandee and Michael. How, I wondered, would Don's perspective be different if he were lying in a hospital room attached to a chemotherapy machine? How might a bout of cancer strip his illusions or clarify what his true personal needs were? How might

Don be getting his "house in order" before he dies? When confronted by a few friends trying to prevent his marriage derailment, Don played the God-loves-me-and-will-forgive-me card. God wants Don to be happy, right? And his wife and kids to be miserable? Play that one out.

I walked away from that awkward encounter feeling two major emotions: First, there but for the grace of God go I. Second, I felt sorry to see how blinded Don was by his own brokenness. By justifying his behavior and rationalizing his sin, playing the card of what Dietrich Bonhoeffer called "cheap grace," my friend seemed to conveniently forget Jesus' stinging words in the Sermon on the Mount, that other part of the gospel where Jesus says "I never knew you. Depart from me you who practice lawlessness" (Matt. 7:23). Pascal wrote, "Truly it is an evil to be full of faults, but it is a still greater evil to be full of them, and to be unwilling to recognize them." Philip Yancey points out that people tend to divide into two categories: the righteous and the guilty. But in the story of the woman caught in adultery, Jesus flips the tables on our self-righteous religious categorizations.

> In a brilliant stroke Jesus replaces the two assumed categories, righteous and guilty, with two different categories: sinners who admit and sinners who deny. The woman caught in adultery helplessly admitted her guilt. Far more problematic were people like the Pharisees who denied or repressed guilt.[8]

Whether our brokenness comes from the physical infirmity of chronic illness or the seductive nature of our own sin or heinous acts of sin committed against us, the Scripture makes clear that we need to admit we live in a broken world and that we are all broken. But in our brokenness, we don't see how blind we really are. We are oblivious to our own wrecking-ball behavior, and everyone can see the chinks in our armor but us. In the brokenness of our addictive proclivity to sin, we break our vows to God, our spouses, our children, and our friends.

> God is always waiting, always first initiating his willingness to reach out to us in our brokenness.

It is for our brokenness that Christ came to forgive our sin, remove our guilt, heal our wounds, and restore us to a loving relationship with the Father. But for him to do that, we must admit our need. Just as a child falls on the playground and cries out for help, we need to admit that we have fallen and cry out to our Father for help. God is always waiting, always first initiating his willingness to reach out to us in our brokenness. "This is love: not that we loved God, but that he loved us and sent his Son as an atoning sacrifice for our sins" (1 John 4:10).

The Psalms affirm God's tenderness for the brokenhearted. Just like a dad scooping up his child with a scraped knee, God eagerly desires to save those with scraped hearts and staggering spirits. "The LORD is close to the brokenhearted and saves those who are crushed in spirit" (34:18). "A broken spirit; a broken and contrite heart, O God, you will not despise" (51:17). "He heals the brokenhearted and binds up their wounds" (147:3).

I was just writing in my journal this morning about how accustomed I am to tolerating and moderating my sin before God. I am more apt to play God's grace card than make a detailed, heartfelt confession of my sin. In my own brokenness, I am tempted to justify, minimize, and rationalize my self-deception. My friend Bob Munck, a recovering addict, says that denial means "Don't Even kNow I Am Lying." Sometimes our circumstances are so confusing and our pain so blinding that we don't even know how to articulate what our heart is trying to say to us. We don't understand why God is allowing pain in our lives or why he hasn't freed us from a habitual sin.

In times like these, we have to slow down and remind ourselves whose we are. We need friends and companions in Christ to speak to us about the truth of whose we are. To remind us of our true identity in Christ. In *The Sacrament of the Present Moment*, Jean-Pierre De Caussade writes,

> Is not a picture painted on a canvas by the application of one stroke of the brush at a time? Similarly the cruel chisel destroys a stone with each cut. But what the stone suffers by repeated blows is no less the shape the mason is making of it. And should a poor stone be asked, "What is happening to you?" it might reply "Don't ask me. All I know is that for my part there is nothing for me to know or do, only to remain steady under the hand of my master

and to love him and suffer him to work out my destiny. It is for him to know how to achieve this. I know neither what is best and most perfect, and I suffer each cut of the chisel as though it were the best thing for me, even though, to tell the truth, each one is my idea of ruin, destruction and defacement. But, ignoring all this, I rest contented with the present moment. Thinking only of my duty to it, I submit to the work of this skillful master without caring to know what it is."[9]

What is God doing at this moment in your life?
Don't ask me.
That's one of the most brilliant responses of authentic faith I've ever heard.

Whatever your pain, problem, or predicament, God promises to make something beautiful out of your brokenness. Even if you can't see it right now, let the chips fall where they may as you cling to your Father as his child. Jesus, your broken Savior, understands your brokenness like no one else. His cross is the ultimate picture of broken wholeness. And it is on this cross that he died for cancer patients and adulterers, alcoholics and drug addicts, Sunday school teachers and stock brokers, country club presidents and codependents, pornographers and poets, truckers and tortilla makers, pastors and priests, prisoners and prima ballerinas, Wall Street bankers and writers with wrist pain. We don't need to know what God is doing. What we need to know is that God loves us and Jesus died for us all. If we allow it, our brokenness will bring us ever closer to our Father as we abandon our lives to him.

We must accept our brokenness to find our wholeness in Christ.

And in the midst of our brokenness, God will help us deal with our fear.

SEVEN

What If vs. What Is

I've been surfing for over twenty years, but I still have to force myself to go out in twelve-foot surf. Every August and into the early fall when hurricanes form off the tip of Baja, California, if those black and white cotton candy swirls head a couple hundred miles west into a meteorological sweet spot known as the "swell window," surfers up and down the Southern California coast can count on large incoming swells for all southern facing beaches. Since the average hurricane produces enough energy to power Los Angeles for a few days, each new storm is met with an electrical mix of fear, excitement, wonder, and awe. News of a hurricane off Baja and overhead surf generates a buzz in the air for what spots will be best, and work schedules are rearranged, tides checked, and suspicious wives hear the words, "I've got a board meeting at 6:00 a.m. tomorrow."

I love to surf with my buddies who share my appreciation for the indescribable beauty of long, glassy waves and the raw physical power of the ocean when God decides to play in the bathtub. Put me in four- to six-foot surf and I'm stoked to catch a few fun waves. But when the surf picks up to double overhead, my mind can easily saturate itself with an undertow of anxiety and churning riptides full of fear. Next to electrocution, drowning is one of my least favorable ways to die. I don't like the idea of human flotsam.

So when the cotton candy started swirling off Baja a couple weeks ago, I steeled myself for what was to be the biggest, cleanest, most epic surf in five years. The surf had been pretty weak all summer, so there was nothing anyone could really do to prepare for the big surf but to go for it. You just paddle out and take your lumps as they come. The only problem is that each lump is a hurricane-generated, 10- to 12-foot monster pushing enough water to fill 10 Olympic-size swimming pools, each gallon weighing 8.31 pounds. Kind of like God hosing off his driveway. Take that on the head.

Anonymous said, "The rule for overcoming fear is to head right into it," and that's exactly what my buddy John and I did when we paddled out early one Monday morning off Cotton's Point, where Richard Nixon had lived with a white-water view of the Pacific. It was a solid eight to ten feet on the sets, which meant an occasional double-overhead set was sure to spank us when least expected. I had butterflies in my stomach the size of seagulls, but I kept my fear in check by occasionally slapping myself.

The sun was just breaking through the clouds off the sage-colored mountains of Camp Pendleton as our arms stroked a steady rhythm through the cool, glassy water. The lineup at Cotton's was packed with more than sixty guys in the water. Not only did we have to contend with big waves, we were now running a human slalom course. Don't get me wrong here. I love dropping in on a large Cotton's wave as it peaks and lines up, wrapping up toward the beach. There's nothing better than carving up and down its broad face, hoping the inside section will throw a quick barrel. What's no fun though is getting caught inside during a long lineup, taking wave after wave on the head. Ask my buddies, I'm a master at getting pile-driven while paddling back out.

John and I had been in the water for over an hour. We'd each caught a few waves, but with the peak shifting to the north and south on the set waves, the pickings were slim. The sets were arriving every fifteen to twenty minutes, so we just talked, told jokes, and laughed, part of the fun of sitting in the lineup with friends. We were the farthest outside, waiting to pick off the largest waves, which also translates that we didn't want to get hammered on the next set like the poor slobs on the inside.

All of a sudden, black shadows surfaced in the far distance, approaching us like storm troopers in the night. I hoped I was hallucinating, perhaps envisioning an air-craft carrier or two passing by, but from past beatings, I knew better. John and I began digging for the horizon, reaching out and pulling each stroke in as hard and as fast as we could. The pack behind us followed like a school of fish, pumping toward the building, monolithic incoming set. When a big set approaches, it doesn't matter how fast you're paddling, it never seems fast enough. If you're in the right spot, you can get over them. If you're not, you better be ready to become the next Jacque Cousteau.

John and I climbed up and over the tall dark face of the first wave. Easily twelve feet high. Lungs pumping, I kept paddling as hard and as fast as I could. The next wave was bigger and farther out than the first one. "C'mon, c'mon!" I muttered under my breath, know-ing if I didn't get over this one, I was going to have a lunch date with Turtle from *Finding Nemo*. The second wave lumbered toward us in a massive liquid arch, and John and I barely scratched over it. We were grateful for a second until we saw what was next. By our best estimation, the third and final wave of the set began breaking about ten miles offshore. Well, that's how far it felt. The next wave, the largest wave of the set, at least fifteen feet high. We were about halfway up it when its fat lip began to crumble, cascading down like a white fluid avalanche. Sliding off my nine-foot long board, I pushed the board up the face of the wave and dove through the stomach of the churning leviathan. John did the same. A couple seconds later, we both punched out the back of the beast. As we surfaced, we let out a simultaneous hoot expressing our mutual gratefulness for escaping the depths below.

Climbing back on our boards, we watched the wave stampede toward shore like an angry bull. Spray and mist filled the air, the morning light glowing through in subtle yellow hues. Tiny black orbs popped to the foamy surface of the frothing water. *Those would be human heads*, I said to myself as I caught my breath while resting on my board. Caught inside the three-wave set, over fifty surfers looked like jettisoned cargo, a veritable garage sale of scattered surfboards and broken leashes. John and I barely missed the wrath of this monster. The sea was calm again. The walls in front of me were gone, and so were my fears. God was finished hosing off his driveway.

What If?

Like a large incoming wall of water ready to hold you down so long you feel as if your lungs are going to explode, fear comes in all shapes and sizes. But the most obvious fears we have, such as for our physical safety—drowning in high surf or stalling our car on railroad tracks or coming down with a life-threaten-

> The fears we face today, the ones lurking in our hearts that seem to play a continual game of hide-and-seek with our emotions, are rooted in our longing to be chosen, loved, and accepted.

ing disease—are quite different from the invisible fears that do more damage to our hearts on a daily basis. The deepest fears we battle are far more embarrassing to share with another person than a fear of heights or small, crowded spaces or stepping on an airplane. The fears we face today, the ones lurking in our hearts that seem to play a continual game of hide-and-seek with our emotions, are rooted in our longing to be chosen, loved, and accepted. Our fears are rooted in those two small words that get blown up into terrifying proportions: *What if?*

We all have our own "what ifs." The person who tells you they have no fear lives with the fear of appearing weak or vulnerable. Fear is a core component of the broken human condition. Tell me, what are your what ifs? What kind of bad place does your heart go to when faced with uncertainty, loss, or sudden change? What are the voices of fear you hear whispering in your heart?

What if I fail?

What if I don't make the right choice?

What if this big business deal doesn't come through?

What if people don't want to get close to me once they get to know me?

What if others take advantage of me or abandon me?

What if I don't get married or am always alone?

What if I can't perform to the high standards I set for myself?

What if I can't find a new father or mother for my children?

What if my spouse isn't faithful to me?

What if I never overcome this addiction?

What if I'm always in pain?

What if I lose my job and can't provide for my family?

What if the dreams I have for my life don't come true?

What if I lose control and everything falls apart?

What if people ignore me or don't pay attention to me?

What if I don't achieve the success and riches I think I deserve?

What if I take a bullet for speaking up?

What if I don't get the recognition, admiration, and praise I need?

What if I share a secret with a friend or co-worker and they use it against me?

What if I never measure up to the expectations of others?

What if my worst fears come true?

What if God finally has enough of me?

Our what ifs are often stronger than the reality of what is true. What ifs are the fears birthed out of past wounds and rejections that we wrestle with in the present and project into the future. What ifs paralyze our thinking, cloud our judgment, and cut us off from the truth of who God says we already are. What ifs are the lies of Satan designed to derail us from the path of faith by causing us to fixate on Murphy's Law that "whatever can go wrong, will go wrong." The fears associated with our what ifs are always experienced in the present moment, not in the past, and as Merton noted, they are the fruit of unanswered questions about our future.

What ifs are fear's best friends. They trigger all manner of volatile emotions. When you feel tired, burned out, overwhelmed, lonely, or scared, what other emotions hop on board the terror train? When fear runs rampant in your heart, you will feel insecure, rejected, unloved, left out, snowed under, intimidated, controlled, anxious, manipulated, suspicious, confused, angry, worthless, ashamed, unforgiven.

> What ifs are fear's best friends. They trigger all manner of volatile emotions.

What do you suppose could happen in our lives if we started to live out of the truth of *what is* instead of living within the paralyzing and confining fears of *what if*? Our fears will always attempt to overwhelm us, and just like a surfer duck-diving through the face of a large oncoming wave, we need to punch through our fears. Fear will keep us out of the water and out of life if we allow it. If we allow fear to rule in our hearts, our lives will be filled with page after page of what ifs, each fear drowning out the tender voice of our heavenly Father who longs for us to hear the reassuring words of his presence, "Do not be afraid, for I am with you" (Gen. 26:24).

These are the same words that have been spoken to the same trouble-hearted people like you and me for centuries throughout the pages of Scripture. Take Moses, the stuttering, Egyptian-killing, fear-filled shepherd on the lam whom God spoke to from a burning bush. God called him on a mission to rescue the Israelites from Egypt, and Moses asked for an immediate decommission. You remember the story.

What Is?

Averse to risk, Moses punctuates every other word to God with his worries and apprehensions. "Who am I that I should go to Pharaoh?" "Suppose the Israelites won't listen to me, then what?" "What if Pharaoh won't listen to me or what if they don't believe me or what if they say the Lord didn't appear to me?"

What if? What if? What if?

Clear in his calling of Moses, God cuts him off and gives him a reality check.

"Moses, what is in your hand?"

Moses is carrying his shepherd's staff, a tool that has served him well for years.

"Throw it on the ground," God tells him.

Moses drops his staff on the ground, and the staff slithers into a snake. God tells him to grab the tail of the sidewinder, and lo, the snake straightens back into his staff. Then another miracle from God, this time a disappearing leprosy hand trick. But Moses' fears are still rattling his cage, and he grovels before God.

"God, I'm kinda slow with this stuttering problem. Please send somebody else."

God's anger burns toward Moses and his repeated attempts to march through the Chicken Exit. Aaron is enlisted to speak on Moses' behalf. God promises to show them both what to say, how to say it, and when to say it. Before leaving the burning bush, God's final words to Moses are, "And don't forget your staff." If I were God, I would have left in a huff, at least blowing some sand in Moses' eyes.

Moses' heart reeks with fear. His fears smell worse than the Nile marshes at low tide. And who wouldn't be afraid? God is asking him to bankrupt the Egyptian economy by leading the entire Egyptian workforce, millions of Israelite slaves, out into some far off La-La Promised Land. Moses is a fugitive, runaway royalty wanted back in the kingdom for first-degree murder. But what is God's response? Did God say forget it—I'll get someone else who isn't such a wuss? Does he let Moses back out to a safe, comfortable existence to live with his father-in-law picking fleas off sheep? With a powerful compassion, God looks beyond Moses' fears by helping him see what he can't see.

"Moses, what is in your hand?"

"My staff, Lord?"

God takes Moses past his fears of *what if* by asking him *what is.*

What is, not *what if,* anchors our heart in the truth of who we are before God. Despite all of our fears, rational or not, what is truest about who we are is that we are the chosen, loved, and accepted children of God. We are not the sum of all our fears. Nor the pain of all our brokenness. Nor the heartbreaking history left scattered behind us. Nor the future we fear ahead of us. What is truest is God's love for us and the power he makes available to us to overcome our deepest fears. Asking "What is true?" is the operative question of a child of God. "What is true?" is always the question to follow "Whose am I?" By knowing whose we are and what is true, we can move out of the darkness of our fears and into the light of God's penetrating love.

Whether consciously or subconsciously, we think before we feel. Our feelings and subsequent fears flow out of what we think about. To live and walk in the light of God's love requires our choice, our cooperation with the Holy Spirit, in the daily, sometimes moment-by-moment, renewing of our minds. To smash through the looming wall of fear, we need to remind ourselves of the truth of who God is, the truth of whose we are, and the truth about the challenges before us. Renewing our minds is an essential daily practice if we are going to chase the screaming monkeys of fear out of our hearts.

"Finally, brothers, whatever is true, whatever is noble, whatever is right, whatever is pure, whatever is lovely, whatever is admirable—if anything is excellent or praiseworthy—think about such things" (Phil. 4:8).

Since we live in a broken world in which bad and scary things do happen, it is vitally important to know how and where fear grabs hold of our heart. Knowing whose we are as children of God is the essence of spiritual identity, but it doesn't mean we won't ever be afraid. Knowing that we are beloved and accepted children of God enables us to live with a whole and integrated heart, but we also must be willing to face our fears.

> To smash through the looming wall of fear, we need to remind ourselves of the truth of who God is, the truth of whose we are, and the truth about the challenges before us.

The Divided Kingdom

In Matthew's Gospel, immediately after Jesus heals many people and warns them not to tell anyone who he is, we read again the affectionate words of the Father written long ago by the prophet Isaiah, who foretold of the coming Messiah.

"Here is my servant whom I have chosen, the one I love, in whom I delight" (Matt. 12:18).

There again are those words our hearts need to hear. *Chosen. Loved. Accepted. The object of God's delight.*

Immediately following these words, a blind and mute demon-possessed man is brought before Jesus. Jesus heals the man, restoring his sight and speech before the speechless crowd. The people in the crowd begin to ask if Jesus could really be the Son of David. There is definite confusion concerning his identity and his lineage to King David. The Pharisees jump in to bait Jesus and capitalize on the confusion within the crowd. "It is only by Beelzebub, the prince of demons, that this fellow drives out demons" (Matt. 12:24).

Knowing their thoughts and plans to conspire against him, Jesus says to the Pharisees and for all to hear, "Every kingdom divided against itself will be ruined, and every city or household divided against itself will not stand. If Satan drives out Satan, he is divided against himself. How then can his kingdom stand?" (Matt. 12:25–26). The truth here is that every kingdom divided against itself will fall. That includes the kingdom of our hearts. In John 10:10, Jesus makes it very clear that "the thief comes to steal, kill and destroy." Jesus has come to give us an abundant life far greater than we can ever imagine, but we can never experience the joy and meaning of this life if we live with divided hearts. Any heart or household divided against itself will not stand.

Whatever it takes to divide your heart, Satan wants to rip, tear, separate, and place a wedge between you and God. Call it a spiritual wedgie. Your spiritual enemy wants to split your heart into a divided kingdom by stealing as much space in your heart as possible. Whenever fear takes root or residence in your heart, you are living in a divided kingdom. Every time you listen to the imaginary what ifs of fear, you are listening to the lies of what is not true. Some fears are normal and natural, but any fear that divides your heart against the truth of who you are as a child of God is part of Satan's strategy against you.

> The abundant life is personally experiencing the love of God despite all of our fears and brokenness. It is knowing that whatever happens in this life, nothing can separate us from the love of God.

How come so many Christians don't experience this "abundant life"? Too often, we associate the abundant life with feeling good about ourselves or the myth that Christ came to take away our problems or the belief that God will really love us once we get our act together. No, the abundant life is personally experiencing the love of God despite all of our fears and brokenness. It is knowing that whatever happens in this life, nothing can separate us from the love of God. It is in living a surrendered life in the full knowledge that we are chosen, loved, and accepted. The abundant life is living with hope. It is the breakthrough of peace in the hurricanes of life's problems. Jesus said, "In this world you will have trouble, but take courage, I have overcome the world." The abundant life is walking in friendship with Jesus, the source of all life, and seeing his smile when he looks at you.

Are you free, or is your heart a divided kingdom? Have you experienced the transforming power of the Holy Spirit to free you from everything that keeps you from living as a chosen child of God? Imagine what could be done in your life, what could be accomplished, what could be created, if fear could be overcome? A divided heart leads to a divided kingdom in our day-to-day lives in which we eat and sleep, work and play. But by his goodness and grace, God will move our hearts from the familiarity of fear to the intimate truth of his favor.

Finding the Favor of Your Father

You don't have to earn God's favor. You don't have to search for it or travel the world in a spiritual quest for enlightenment. You don't even have to humbly ask for God's favor—you already have it. Remember that small consumer event that happens once a year, also known as Christmas? The story of the birth of Christ hinges on this transforming truth: The light of God's favor has overcome a world hidden by the darkness of fear. In each movement of the Christmas story, we see simple men and women who experience fear like you and me, but they move out of the darkness of their fears by trusting in the goodness of God and his extravagant favor in their lives.

Though his wife, Elizabeth, was childless, Zechariah overcame his fear by boldly praying for a son well into his golden years. "But the angel said to him: 'Do not be afraid, Zechariah; your prayer has been heard'" (Luke 1:13). Elizabeth overcame her fear by hoping against hope that the Lord would one day take away the shame of her barren womb. Mary overcame her fear and listened to Gabriel's amazing announcement. "Do not be afraid, Mary, you have found favor with God" (Luke 1:30). Joseph overcame his fear of what others might say about his pregnant fiancée and took Mary as his wife. "Joseph son of David, do not be afraid to take Mary home as your wife, because what is conceived in her is from the Holy Spirit" (Matt. 1:20). Terrified of the angel of the Lord, the shepherds overcame their fear by dashing into Bethlehem to see the newborn Messiah. "But the angel said to them, 'Do not be afraid. I bring you good news of great joy that will be for all the people'" (Luke 2:10). Slam-dunking fear in the can, the wise men close the Christmas story by overcoming their fear of Herod by obeying God and returning home by another route.

The Christmas story is ultimately a story of God entering a fear-filled world with a peace so powerful that no obstacle could overcome his favor toward his children. In Christ, peace is offered to all men and women on whom his favor rests. Though we may experience fear from time to time, we no longer live under the rule of fear. We live by the favor of our heavenly Father. He is our *abba*, which is how the Hebrew children called out to their fathers. "For you did not receive a spirit that makes you a slave again to fear, but you received the Spirit of sonship. And by him we cry, '*Abba*, Father'" (Rom. 8:15). Because of God's favor, you can call him "*Abba*, Father, Daddy."

It would be completely ridiculous if any of my four children approached me every day and said, "Daddy, am I really your son? Am I really your daughter?" To constantly question the nature of a relationship is to throw the whole relationship into a dubious territory of instability, insecurity, doubt, and disbelief. In essence, *fear*. No matter what experience you've had with your earthly father, you have the favor of God. He is your *abba*, and he longs for you to know his favor.

Yet as humans, we do fear, and understandably so. We fear because we are born into an unsafe world, and our experience confirms, in varying degrees, that we are surrounded by broken relationships. Some of us were raised in families where security, intimacy, acceptance, and belonging were anything but the norm. Having experienced rejection, isolation, and disappointment in our human relationships, we naturally ask these same questions of our heavenly Father. God, do you love me? Am I accepted? Do I belong? Must I prove myself to you like everyone else? Is your love something to be earned? Are you only happy with me when I don't sin? Can I be broken, filled with sin, and still be loved? Do you still choose me when I question your love? When I'm angry with you? When I run away from you? Do you still choose me, love me, and accept me in spite of myself? When everyone else in my life confirms that I am unworthy of their love, do you still love me? The answer is yes. God knows the longing in your heart. God's answer to your unanswered question of whether or not you are worthy of his love is always yes. Jesus is the yes of God's relentless love for you.

You may have been raised in a home in which it was clear you weren't the "chosen one." But your heavenly Father doesn't treat any of his children this way. "God does not show favoritism" (Rom. 2:11). Webster defines favor as "to approve or like." Let's play these words out. God not only approves of you, he actually likes you. It's one thing to say, "God loves me." God's supposed to love everyone because he's God. That's his job, right? True, the Bible says that "God is love." He cannot *not* love you, but God also likes you. He made you. He knows you. It gives him great pleasure to love you because you are his child.

Not only does God like you, Nouwen writes, but his choosing of you is inclusive and not at the exclusion of others. God is partial to all of his children. With the favor and approval of your heavenly Father, you no longer have to walk in fear. You no longer need to seek the favor of your boss, co-workers, professors, clients, family members, or friends. You no longer need to seek the favor of your mother or father who, in their brokenness, are unable to offer you the acceptance you long for.

Fear is a very real part of the spiritual journey. The fear and anxiety of the future can only be declawed by a courageous commitment to live in the unconditional love of God today. We don't need to minimize our fears or pretend they don't exist. We just need to recognize them for what they are and how they first took root in our heart. Instead of making fear the enemy, we can befriend it by allowing it to remind us whose we are. Fear then becomes a gift, redeemed by God and used by God to accomplish his purpose in our lives as we surrender our fears to him.

When I'm struggling and feeling overwhelmed with fear, a good friend reminds me of the two basic choices before me. I can . . . Forget Everything And Run. Or I can . . . Face Everything And Recover. On my good days, with a little encouragement from Paul, I choose the latter. The surf is not always as big as it looks.

"For God did not give us a spirit of timidity (of cowardice, of craven, cringing and fawning fear), but of power and of love and of calm and well-balanced mind and discipline and self-control" (2 Tim. 1:7 AMP).

What, then, does it take to actually live as a chosen, loved, and accepted child of God? How can you live an authentic spiritual life without making it seem like another item to check off on an already packed to-do list? How do you go from listening to the voices of fear to listening to the voice of God?

What's the secret? There is no secret.

You follow the way of Jesus.

EIGHT

The Way of Jesus

Whump! Whump! Whump! It's 6:30 in the morning. As I step onto the treadmill at 24 Hour Fitness, I feel like I am slogging through a minefield. My still-asleep senses are being bombarded with a surround-sound, shock and awe noise campaign of contemporary culture. I haven't even wiped the sleep from my eyes, but I am in the bull's-eye of an audio concussion. Above me are black speakers thumping and whumping hip-hop music, urging me to feel the beat. The detonations are deafening. I can feel the beat, all right. I haven't even begun to pound my body, but the blaring music is pummeling me. *Bump-bump-bump! Whump-whump-whump!*

As I program my treadmill for a forty-minute walk, I see before me seven ceiling-mounted televisions all tuned to different stations. This place looks more like NASA mission control than a gym. I can't hear a single word from any of the early morning shows, CNN broadcasts, MTV, the Home and Garden Network, but all are lip-syncing their voices to me. Each one is clamoring for my attention. I can read the ticker tape running on the bottom of the screens, but some of those words get jumbled, which makes for an interesting game trying to follow the garbled monologue. I am walking on a treadmill being blasted with throbbing, unintelligible music as I try to watch seven televisions simultaneously. I feel nauseous. I should be walking on a long, quiet beach.

That beach is only a mile away.

How much distance separates you from hearing the voice of God in your life?

Brand-Name Noise

My experience at the gym is no different than yours. All around us, you and I live with pure, unadulterated brand-name noise. All the noise in our culture, all the voices we hear each and every day, in large part, are designed to distract and deafen our ears to the voice of God. It is part of the cosmos Jesus spoke of: a world system set against the ways of God. A world in rebellion, as evidenced in famine, disease, economic inequality, racism, hate, war, and rumors of war. Entertainment is one specific way our culture has developed to cope with the harshness of this world in order to numb our pain and the reality of how the rest of the world lives. Activity is another way to numb our pain. We are activity addicts. You may not be in Alcoholics Anonymous, but you may be a card-carrying member of AAA—Activity Addicts Anonymous. We get so much praise for how much we achieve, but what we really need is a support group to teach us to slow down.

Our spiritual impoverishment and inability to realize who we are as the children of God, I believe, is due in large part to our overeating at the fast-food activity counter of American culture. We suffer from a compulsive disorder of blindly binging on whatever our culture serves, not stopping to consider whether or not what we are consuming has any dietary value to our souls. We turn on the television and radio to shatter the silence. We are afraid to be alone with our thoughts. We numb our hearts and minds with the Novocain of our noisy brand-name world. We prefer the escapist illusions of "reality" TV or the Internet to God's beauty all around us. And here, I am speaking of the church, the body of Christ, and not the culture at large. Spiritual transformation must begin with the people of God who choose to live by the path of grace, listening for the voice of God instead walking in lockstep on the treadmill of our noisy culture.

To walk this path of grace, we must stop and consider how much we are bombarded with the Next Big Thing.

The Next Best Brand. Think for a minute what a "brand" really is. Ranchers use a burning hot branding iron to sear their mark of ownership on their cattle and sheep. The unique brand names the animal. It is a sign of identity and ownership. The whole goal of advertising is to direct your purchasing decisions by providing you with specific brand-name identities to define who you are by what you wear and what you own. You are being branded and sweet-talked to switch brands. You are being named and renamed. *I am a Coke drinker. You are a Pepsi drinker. I'm a Pepper . . . you're a Pepper.*

What matters most is not *what* you identify with but *who* you identify with. Who you identify with will determine how you see yourself. Who you identify with is a profound question of spiritual identity, and that question finds its essence in what is truly in your heart. But the real issue here is not brand names or stuff. Jesus said it's not what's outside a man's heart that makes him unclean but what flows from inside his heart that makes him unclean. If your heart is clean, knock yourself out. Wear Versace or Ralph Lauren or Quiksilver. What matters most is your heart, who you ultimately identify with, and whose name you bear. "The LORD does not look at the things man looks at. Man

> What matters most is not *what* you identify with but *who* you identify with. Who you identify with will determine how you see yourself.

looks at the outward appearance, but the LORD looks at the heart" (1 Sam. 16:7).

If we are going to grow in Christ as the chosen, loved, and accepted children of God, we have to name the competing voices in our life for what they are. We have to ask ourselves what brand names are competing for our true name and true identity as children of God. Our spiritual identity is stunted when we place an overemphasis on materialism and the brand names paraded before us. We will never find true security, comfort, belonging, and attachment in the Next New Thang. Our true security is in God.

Brand names aside, what other names seek to usurp or rival your true name as a child of God? What names from the past still haunt you and challenge who you are? What negative, self-defeating names are known to you and you alone? What names have shamed you? What names have you assumed to compensate and fill the hole in your heart? What heartbreaking labels were given to you by others who didn't love you as God loved you then and loves you now: Loser, Rebel, Liar, Peacemaker, Drunk, Clown, Problem Child, Hypocrite, Seducer, Performer, Loner, Slut, Star, Addict. Whatever you have been named by the brokenness of others or however you have named yourself, you were made to live in the fullness of your true name . . . you know your true name by now, don't you?

As a Father whom you can fully trust, God has provided you with very specific ways to live out a childlike faith in him. Each one of these ways is the mark of being a disciple of Jesus. Jesus said, "I am the way and the truth and the life. No man comes to the Father except through me" (John 14:6). If you're going to live a deep, satisfying life as a chosen child of God, you have to know the way you're going. You have to know and experience the way, the truth, and the life of Jesus. It is through the way of Jesus that you find your way to the Father. What then are the ways of a child of God? What characterizes the life of one who is chosen, loved, and accepted?

The Way of Relationship

The way of Jesus is the way of relationship. As you read through the Gospels, the one major theme that is impossible to miss is the way Jesus loves to spend time with his Father. Jesus has been named by his Father, and this is the primary relationship he pursues throughout the course of his life. We learn how to be in relationship with the Father through the example of Jesus, the chosen, loved, and accepted Son of God. We grow in intimacy with the Father by following and modeling how Jesus interacted with his Father.

If you want to experience true spiritual transformation, knowing God the Father is all about developing a deeper relationship with him. It is not about ascribing to a particular denominational theological position. Nor is it a particular set of legalistic behaviors that make you a "good" Christian as opposed to "bad" Christians who watch

R-rated movies, drink alcohol, and cut in line at the cash register during a half-annual sale at Nordstrom's. No, knowing God is a relationship based on love that flows from the heart. Jesus loved his father from the heart, and this is how we are called to love God.

> If you want to experience true spiritual transformation, knowing God the Father is all about developing a deeper relationship with him.

From the very beginning of his ministry to the final hours in the Garden of Gethsemane before his capture that led to the cross, Jesus pursues his relationship with his Father by spending time alone with him. To know anybody takes both quantity and quality time. When by himself, Jesus talks with his father just like any son would do. Take a peek here . . .

Very early in the morning, while it was still dark, Jesus got up, left the house and went off to a solitary place, where he prayed.

Mark 1:35

At daybreak Jesus went out to a solitary place.

Luke 4:42

After he had dismissed them, he went up on a mountainside by himself to pray. When evening came, he was there alone.

Matthew 14:23

He said to them, "Sit here while I go over there and pray."

Matthew 26:36

There is no substitute for prayer—simply listening and talking to God—for deepening your relationship with your heavenly Father. In prayer and in meditating on God's Word, we discover who God is and who we are in relationship to him. By prayer, we rediscover *whose* we are. Prayer reorients us to the truth of God and our true identity in Christ. Prayer quiets the many voices and false names competing for attention in our lives. Prayer is simple conversation with God, motivated by the Holy Spirit at work in our hearts, drawing us to a greater life of worship toward the one who loves us like no other.

We pray because Jesus prayed. Through prayer, Jesus persevered through challenges, overcame temptation, received strength, and surrendered his life to the perfect will of his Father. Prayer doesn't need to be complicated, wordy, or religious sounding. It simply needs to be honest. Heartfelt. Authentic and true to where we are at in the present moment.

Whether it's a few minutes locked in the bathroom away from screaming kids, a short walk through a quiet park, or getting up before everyone else in your home, give yourself the gift of spending time alone with God to deepen your relationship with him. Spending time alone with God in prayer is the basis for an ongoing conversation with him throughout the day.

146

On the days when I allow busyness and misplaced priorities to shortcut time alone with God, I can see a difference in my attitude and how I respond to people and situations. When I do take the time to pray or read Scripture or reflect on a particular devotional writing, everything else seems to wrap around that time. But when I get busy doing other things and don't pray, I always miss the time I could have spent in prayer. Prayer is not an obligation; it's a privilege to talk with someone who loves to connect with my heart.

The Way of Rest

"Daddy, why do you write so much and never play with us anymore?"

Ouch. It was Christmastime, and I was submerged in a flood of words and ideas as I thrashed toward a book deadline. If Joseph and Mary had come knocking at my door to see if there was any room at the inn, I probably would have tossed them pocket change and told them to check Motel 6. That is essentially the short shrift Krista and the kids were getting as I sequestered myself upstairs in my office during Christmas vacation.

I looked up from the computer as if my dive mask had been pulled off in a hundred feet of water. Ellie, six years old at the time, stood at the edge of my desk like Cindy Lou Who with her long blond curls, wondering why I was such a Grinch.

What I wanted to do was give my best Jim Carrey Grinch impersonation and scream, "Oh, the audacity . . . the unmitigated gall! Can't this child see I am *creating*?" Frankly, at six years old, Ellie doesn't give a rip about what I create. At six years old, Ellie could care less whether I'm a writer, a checkout clerk at Costco, an electrical engineer, or a movie star. All she wants is time with Dad. She, like any other child, is more concerned with the pressing questions of the moment: Will you play with me? Did you remember to get my Coco Puffs? Are we still going to the movies like you promised? Will you read me a story? Am I going to get a bicycle for Christmas?

Work consumes so much of our time and emotional energy that if we do not build times of rest and renewal, we will deprive ourselves of the opportunity to live as children of God. When we are exhausted, tired, anxious, and preoccupied with the sheer task of our work, we then place ourselves in a precarious position of not being available to give others the gift of being chosen, loved, and accepted. If we are to have an active and purposeful life marked by the love of God, we must actively pursue a life of rest.

We need to detach and disengage from our addiction to activity. We must let go of our preoccupation with what is most pressing. Leave our love affair with the immediacy of technology. Abandon, or at least identify, what we want versus what we need. We must regularly and intentionally kick out the two-by-fours propping up all the outer attachments of our False Self that shape the illusion we

believe to be our True Self. Rest is a time for us to come
to our senses to remember whose we are. When we know
whose we are, we discover who we are. This is when life
becomes a bit clearer.

When you began this book, you read about me sitting
in LAX with my heart in a very ugly place of burnout and
exhaustion. But Jesus offers you and me a better way. It
is the way of rest. Rest is God's design for restoring our
heart to hear the voice of his love. From the very creation of the world, God designed rest to be the rhythm
and integral pattern of life. After creating the world in
six days, on the seventh day God rested. When you and I
don't rest, we are one day ahead of God, metaphorically
speaking. We are to follow God, not lead him with our
agenda. He does not play "follow the leader."

Jesus' invitation of rest is open to all who choose to
respond to the Father's call of restoration of the heart.
"Come to me, all you who are weary and burdened, and
I will give you rest. Take my yoke upon you and learn
from me, for I am gentle and humble in heart, and you
will find rest for your souls. For my yoke is easy and my
burden is light" (Matt. 11:28–29).

The rest Jesus provides is true soul rest. David wrote in
Psalm 62:1, "My soul finds rest in God alone; my salvation
comes from him." Where does your soul find its rest?
When you are exhausted from the stress and pressure
of life, does your heart find the deep soul rest it needs?
Jesus invites us to unload the burden of our problems,
our pride, our sin and shame, our pain and brokenness,

our troubled marriages, our conflicts with co-workers, family, or friends. He invites us to bring our weariness and the tired old names we bear to him so that we may hear and be reminded of our true name. When we rest in Jesus and reflect on his life-giving words in Scripture, we just may be reminded of his words to us in John 15: "I no longer call you servants, because a servant does not know his master's business. Instead, I have called you friends, for everything that I learned from my Father I have made known to you" (John 15:15).

> It is never too late to start living as a child of God by resting in him. Are you willing to let that truth penetrate the core of your heart?

Everything Jesus has learned from his Father he wants to make known to you, and sometimes all you need to hear is the still, small voice of Jesus whispering in your heart, "Psst, you're my friend." Jesus calls you his friend, and you are not made to bear the burdens of this life alone. Wearing a heavy yoke by yourself and trying to pull an oxcart filled with guilt, confusion, fatigue, grief, pain, and remorse only sends you into a spiritual tailspin. Jesus invites you to hook up to the yoke of his friendship and the companionship of his father. By resting in him, allowing his grace to lighten whatever is weighing down your heart, you travel the easier way of rest.

It is never too late to start living as a child of God by resting in him. Are you willing to let that truth penetrate the core of your heart? Are you going to allow a divorce to keep you from receiving the love of God? Are you going to allow an addiction to keep you from receiving the kiss of the Father? Are you going to allow self-hatred to keep you from your Father's embrace? Resting in the love of Jesus is the true soul rest your heart longs for.

When we rest, we are doing something vitally important . . . resting! Rest is so intricately tied to listening to the voice of God; we cannot avoid the urgency of taking rest seriously. Keeping the Sabbath day, or any day, holy is God's command to rest and recognize that he is Lord of all. Restoration comes from listening to God by ourselves and in the community of worship God has provided for us in the body of Christ.

Because of their hard, callous hearts, the people of Israel severed their relationship with God and chose not to follow his command to rest. The writer of Hebrews reminds us to make the effort to listen to God's plan for rest and not follow the example of the Israelites.

> "Today, if you hear his voice,
> do not harden your hearts."

For if Joshua had given them rest, God would not have spoken later about another day. There remains, then, a Sabbath-rest for the people of God; for anyone who enters God's rest also rests from his own work, just as God did from his. Let us, therefore, make every effort

to enter that rest, so that no one will fall by following
their example of disobedience

Hebrews 4:7–11

The Way of Reflection

Not only is the way of Jesus the way of relationship
and rest, but it is also the way of reflection. Reflection
flows out of rest. Who has time to reflect when they're
living a frantic life? Reflection enhances our relationship with the Father and our relationship with others.
Reflection allows the Spirit of God room to focus and
reorder our lives.

For me, getting away from others and placing myself
in a beautiful physical location dramatically impacts how
I reflect on God and my life. A couple years ago I started
sneaking off to the San Juan Capistrano Mission to get
alone with God near the bubbling fountains and in the gardens, quiet chapels, and ruins of the Great Stone Church.
After grabbing a cup of coffee and a scone at Diedrich, a
coffeehouse right across the street, I've found that I can't
get away from what the beauty of mission grounds does
for my soul. The mission is a place for solitude and rest
in my journey to live as one who is chosen, loved, and accepted. It is a place for me to detach from my busy roles
as husband, father, friend, pastor, and writer. I detach so
I can rest and attach to the one who calls me by my true
name. I don't know about you, but my outer life quickly

loses focus on its ultimate purpose if my inner life does not have a regular rhythm of rest and reflection.

> Quiet may be the greatest need in our society. Most of us are overscheduled, and the part of life most often neglected is the time for reflection with God. Jesus developed the strong rhythm of time alone, time with a few, and time with the crowds. For us, that rhythm could be time alone with God, time with our families and friends, and time with our work.[10]

Living as a child of God requires a definite degree of boldness, which is why so few people actually choose the reflective life. Living a life of reflection is hard work. It takes courage to step up to God and say as David said,

> Examine me, GOD, from head to foot,
>   order your battery of tests.
> Make sure I'm fit
>   inside and out
> So I never lose
>   sight of your love,
> But keep in step with you,
>   never missing a beat.
>
> Psalm 26:2–3 Message

David isn't the only one who is calling us to live a life of reflection. Jeremiah wrote, "Let us examine our ways and test them, and let us return to the LORD" (Lam. 3:40). Paul tells the Corinthians, "Examine yourselves to see whether you are in the faith; test yourselves" (2 Cor. 13:5).

The rest Jesus offers us is always about returning to God and reorienting our faith to find our true identity in Christ. When we reflect on our lives by examining our hearts, we put ourselves in the very best position to hear the heart of God speak to us. In reflecting, we move from our head to our heart by asking God, "Lord, how is my heart today? Do I love you with all my heart, soul, mind, and strength? In what areas of my life am I withholding my love for you? Am I playing any games of spiritual hide-and-seek with you? And how am I loving others? How is your Spirit evident in my life through how I show others your love, joy, peace, patience, kindness, goodness, faithfulness, and self-control? Am I living for the approval of others or am I passively living disengaged from others out of fear of being hurt again? *Abba* Father, show me today how I can live in your freedom, as one who is truly loved and accepted, ready to take bold steps in the adventure of faith you have before me." This is the radical, transformational life available to us that begins with reflecting and listening for God in our hearts.

The Way of Re-Creation

Surprisingly, the way of Jesus is also the way of rec-reation. Nowhere in the Gospels does Jesus say to his disciples, "Now go out and play today," but James does tell us that "every good and perfect gift is from above, coming down from the Father of the heavenly lights" (1:17). In this wonderful life and freedom, God has given us countless gifts, opportunities, and creative activities that he uses in the restoration of our souls. The best gifts flow out of relationship, rest, reflection, and recreation that reflect his goodness, truth, and beauty in our lives. Recreation—play, fun, sports, exercise, creative hobbies—are an essential part of a life of faith that enhance the inner life of the Spirit.

Unfortunately, the society we live in has made an idol out of the God-given gift of recreation. Pleasure and entertainment are our altars of common worship. NFL Sunday pregame shows have a more faithful following than God. Christmas and Easter are celebrations of the next big movie release, not the birth and resurrection of Christ. Extreme sports offer temporary, immediate gratification for adrenaline junkies who don't have something more to live for. Many of our weekends are not characterized by relationship, rest, reflection, and purposeful recreation but fatigue and frustration as we try to cram as much into our schedules as possible. By the time Monday morning arrives, we're exhausted. Our recreation has been not restorative but draining. While there's nothing wrong with watching a favorite sporting event on TV or relaxing by going to a movie, we need to ask ourselves if we are blind consumers of our culture or if our recreation is actually renewing and re-creating us.

Recreation that is truly restorative always creates a clear sense of well-being and centeredness, both physically and spiritually. Recreation, like the word implies, re-creates in us a heart for God that is expressed by a sincere appreciation and gratefulness. One of the key marks of a disciple of Jesus is not only gratefulness for the grace of God but also gratefulness for all the blessings that God gives to us as his children. Everything we do in re-creating our hearts—whether taking a blessed nap, going out for a run, hitting baseballs with our kids, or lingering over a long dinner with friends—offers you and me plenty of opportunity to thank God for the gift of play that reflects his beauty, truth, and goodness in our lives.

So what re-creates your heart and soul? What playful activities, hobbies, and interests do you immerse yourself in to live out a childlike faith in God? How is your time best spent allowing the re-creative work of God to refresh and remind you of whose you are?

This past summer, my kids and I took up painting. We pulled out an old couch from my home office and replaced it with a large table now covered with acrylic and oil paints, vases filled with brushes of all shapes and sizes, oil pastels and paint sticks, linen canvases, three table easels, and one classic standing fold-up easel. For years, I never considered myself an artist, but when I began experimenting with acrylics by mixing colors and slapping them on canvas for the first time since kindergarten, I said to myself, "Me paint . . . why not?" The child of God in me kicked in gear, unafraid of making mistakes and what others might think of my work. The result? Painting has developed a whole new re-creative passion inside of me. What my kids used to call my "office" is now the "studio." I get to paint and play with my kids as we all see the world through colorful new eyes.

As we paint, we are each creating in community. Individually, but together.

We are a picture of the body of Christ.

The chosen, loved, and accepted bride of Christ.

NINE

The Beloved Bride

I began this book with a few thoughts on anxiety and spiritual insecurity by redirecting the often perplexing question of "Who am I?" to the deeper question of *"Whose* am I?" In a world filled with rejection and self-preservation, far too many people live with the unanswered question of whose they really are. No one has told them whose they are, and so they go off in search of "Who am I?" for the rest of their lives. The resulting fruits of these unanswered questions, as Merton noted, are fear, insecurity, self-hatred, and anxiety felt in the deepest parts of one's heart, soul, and mind.

Looking beyond the self-limiting question of "Who am I?" by having the courage to ask "Whose am I?" opens us up to a whole new life we never imagined. By looking beyond ourselves, we gain a whole new vision for our lives. A transforming life of new possibilities and opportunities. When you and I allow God's loving words spoken to Jesus to take residence in our hearts, we discover whose we are. *This is my Son, whom I love; with him I am well pleased.*

These are the most important thirteen words in this book.

Your search for who you are is over.

You are a chosen, loved, and accepted child of God.

That nagging longing in your heart will only be fulfilled in him.

You have the favor of your Father. You are his beloved. You are his delight.

This is the deepest truth of who you are. We swim in a world of wreckage filled with people yearning to hear these words. These are not my words. They are the very words of God written personally to you.

But in God's wonderful design for transforming this world, you have not been given the name—chosen, loved, and accepted—to keep for yourself. You have been given the precious gift of being called the beloved of God in order to give this wonderful gift away. You have been given a whole new spiritual identity in Christ for the purpose of worshiping God and for sharing the transforming unconditional love of your heavenly Father with everyone you meet today. Sharing with others the truth of their chosenness is evidence that you have gratefully received your true name.

I believe with all my heart that the greatest gift we can give to our spouse, our children, our family and friends, and the people we meet and work with every day is the gift of their chosenness. The people in your life and mine know real, authentic, life-giving love when they experience it. And they know exactly what our lack of love looks and feels like by its absence. The challenge of the chosen, loved, and accepted life is to give it away graciously. Generously. Lavishly.

As a precious son or daughter of God, a family member in the body of Christ, you are now a part of something so much grander and more fantastic than any previous dreams or ideas you imagined for yourself. Through the power of the Holy Spirit, the church is Jesus' living presence here on earth, represented by the men and women whose spiritual identity is rooted in Christ. It is through the church, the beloved bride of Christ, that we as Christians speak the truth of whose we are to one another and to the world.

> I believe with all my heart that the greatest gift we can give to our spouse, our children, our family and friends, and the people we meet and work with every day is the gift of their chosenness.

Jesus is the good shepherd, and as his flock we are called to follow and obey him together. "My sheep listen to my voice; I know them, and they follow me. I give them eternal life, and they shall never perish; no one can snatch them out of my hand" (John 10:27–28). In his book *Life Together*, Dietrich Bonhoeffer, a Lutheran pastor and martyr who was executed in a Nazi concentration camp, reflected on the utmost importance of Christians being in community with one another.

> Christianity means community through Jesus Christ and in Jesus Christ. First, we belong to one another only through and in Jesus Christ. A Christian needs others because of Jesus Christ. Second, that a Christian comes to others only through Jesus Christ. Third, in Jesus Christ, we have been chosen from eternity, accepted in time, and united for eternity.[11]

If we need and belong to one another through Christ and if we are truly the chosen, loved, and accepted bride of Christ, then why are so many Christians disconnected from the life of the local church? Why have so many followers of Christ given up on church? Why are there so many isolated sheep trying to do life on their own?

Rejected Sheep

On August 5, 2003, a Dutch-owned ship named the *MV Cormo Express* left Australia for Saudi Arabia with 57,937 sheep aboard. *Baa*. All of the sheep were two-year-old rams bound to have their throats slit in accordance with Islamic custom. Like any sacrificial offering, the rams were supposed to be in perfect condition.

When the sheep arrived a few weeks later, a small problem developed when the Saudi government inspector refused to accept the shipment. The inspector concluded that over 30 percent of the sheep had developed an unattractive virus known as "scabby mouth." Saudi Arabia was not required to accept the sheep if more than 5 percent of the sheep had scabby mouth. Independent veterinarians from the World Animal Health Organization examined the sheep and declared them healthy, but Saudi Arabia accepted only five thousand or so, leaving the remaining 52,000 to find a home in some other country.

Fear and panic over the "diseased" sheep spread. Rejection ran rampant. Jordan wouldn't allow the 11-deck ship into its harbor. Egypt refused to let the *Cormo* through the Suez Canal. Kuwait ran a headline in the *Al Watan* newspaper: "The Ship of Death is in Kuwait." Iran and Pakistan refused to let the sheep pass through Afghanistan. In Iraq, plans were made for the British to distribute the sheep, but the occupation forces didn't have the resources to deal with the animals. Indonesia was afraid the scabby-mouthed Australian sheep would infect their livestock industry. Sri Lanka and East Timor said no.[12] It wasn't until the end of October, after the sheep had spent 3 months packed in poorly ventilated, tightly packed pens in 104-degree temperatures (whew!), that the small East African country of Eritrea agreed to purchase the sheep. The 52,000 sheep finally found a home, but only after being rejected by a mere 57 countries.

How many people, like the 52,000 sheep on the *Cormo Express*, have gone to churches in which they were treated like unclean scabby-mouthed sheep instead of the chosen, loved, and accepted children of God they are? How many people have jumped around from church to church, looking to find a home of love and acceptance, only to encounter the cold stare of criticism? How many people have been raised in broken, dysfunctional homes and desperately went looking to the church for a new home and a new name but found no home and the name of rejection? How many sinners could no longer stay in church and bear the overwhelming burden of pretending they were no longer sinners? Refusing to live a loveless lie or walk in goose-step, guilt-ridden allegiance to the tyranny of legalism, countless people have wandered off in search of a spirituality that is at least emotionally honest and void of the shame inflicted by others.

From time to time, I meet wandering sheep like this who love God but have not yet discovered the richness of living in authentic (not perfect) Christian community. These people love Jesus but have a visceral dislike for church. They haven't rejected God but a loveless religion heavy on law and stingy on grace. They have been wounded by the brokenness of other Christians, and in their own brokenness, they have severed themselves from the body of Christ. Deep inside, they feel a strong longing for connection with others, but they are ambivalent when it comes to trusting another body of Christians. All of this makes for a sad paradox, because Jesus did not come for the perfect but for the imperfect. For sinners, not self-cleaning, stainless steel saints.

I've also met many Christians who are not physically disconnected from the church at all. These people are very active in religious activities—hopping from one church to the next—but they never develop any deep, authentic relationships. They are emotionally and relationally disconnected from the church. They are Christians on the go, but they are really Christians on the run, because they are afraid to let others get close to their hearts. And still, God has compassion on them, as should we, because those who are afraid to connect are emotionally wounded sheep. Christians on the run first need a place of safety, other Christians to love and accept them for who they are, and a gentle challenge to stay connected in one church so their hearts can be healed in relationship with others.

> Whether you are actively engaged in or on the run from the body of Christ, to love Jesus is to love his beloved bride.

So what does all this mean? Whether you are actively engaged in or on the run from the body of Christ, to love Jesus is to love his beloved bride. It means humbly asking yourself, "If Jesus can choose, love, and accept his church with all of its confusing conflicts and contradictions, then who am I not to?" It means loving the church in the same way Jesus did—by laying down your life "just as Christ loved the church and gave himself up for her" (Eph. 5:25). Following Jesus requires that we drop our preconceived expectations of what we think his church should be. We need the Holy Spirit's help to let go of our wounded defenses by pulling the planks out of our own eyes. The body of Christ is the family of God, but is there any family here on earth in which brothers and sisters don't fight?

You cannot live in the body of Christ and not be wounded. Jesus has given us the gift of grace to forgive one another as he has forgiven us, but following Jesus requires a realistic view of one another and a heavy reliance on the Holy Spirit. We have to ask ourselves if our wounds are keeping us from community. Are our wounds keeping us from loving Jesus' beloved bride as he does? I know my wounds have.

After losing the youth ministry job I loved for seven years, I stayed out of ministry for the next seven years. My story of living with chronic pain is more about the wound of rejection than it is about sore wrists. It is about me running from God when I didn't even know I was running. At the bottom of my depression, an intense wrestling match with God took place. I lost. By his grace, God allowed me to go to the pit of my depression to show me the core of my heart. It was a place I couldn't see when I was in control, wanting to make it on my own.

It was only when I let go of my writing career, the very thing that was keeping me in so much chronic pain, that God said to me, "Okay, you're finally ready to see what's

really in your heart. It's time." Like an elevator descend-
ing deep inside a dark mine shaft, God led me to a deep
cavern I'd never visited before. On the wall of my heart
was posted a sign that read Never-Never, and it was all
about refusing to work in the church again. In my pain, I
didn't even know I was a wandering sheep living with the
wound of rejection. What I needed was the restoration of
my heart, a restoration found only in the body of Christ.

Warren Wiersbe once wrote, "We have too many people
who have plenty of medals and no scars." That's why we
need to pull off our bulletproof vests, bear our scars, and
humbly accept one another with all of our inconsistencies
and inadequacies. As the church, we probably look much
more like the broken body of Christ on the cross than the
resurrected, living body of Christ. But God's viewpoint is
different. In Christ, God sees his church as holy, whole,
and spotless, just as Jesus is the spotless Lamb of God.
God does not see you or me or the crabby old lady in the
third pew as diseased, scabby-mouthed sheep. He sees
us as beloved sons and daughters. His children. This is
why we need one another; to speak the truth of whose we
are into each other's lives.

The Table of Togetherness

On the night Jesus was betrayed and abandoned by
his friends, he said to his disciples, "I have eagerly desired to eat this Passover with you before I suffer" (Luke

For the chosen children of God, community is not an option. The Christian life is not meant to be lived alone. When you become a Christian, Jesus places you into his body.

22:15 NASB). At the Passover, Jesus and his disciples shared the table of togetherness. It is a table of warmth, fellowship, and community, a foreshadowing of his kingdom coming in the life of his church. An indelible picture that Jesus has chosen us and that we are his friends. Jesus eagerly desires to walk with us, and he eagerly desires for us to walk together in community to show the world his love. Whenever we break bread with one another in fellowship, we share the table of togetherness, a poignant reminder that Jesus is always eager to be with us.

The table of togetherness is God's design for you to experience and enjoy sharing life with other brothers and sisters in Christ. Jesus prepares a meal each day that he eagerly awaits to share with us as we share with one another. For the chosen children of God, community is not an option. The Christian life is not meant to be lived alone. When you become a Christian, Jesus places you into his body. The Lord's Supper is the remembrance and celebration of Christ's body and blood shed for our sins; it is the table of togetherness shared by the body of Christ to celebrate the risen Lord. You can't fly solo with God. You can't go it alone.

Living disconnected from the body of Christ or hopping around from church to church limits the transforming work of the Holy Spirit in our lives. It is in community that we encourage and support one another in our walk with Christ. It is in community that we practice living radically different than this competitive, ruthless world bent on trampling over one another to get to the top of the heap. This is where we learn to choose, love, and accept one another. By this, all people will undeniably know we are Jesus' disciples. The body of Christ is where we gather around the table of togetherness to listen carefully to Jesus' words in John 15.

"As the Father has loved me, so have I loved you. Now remain in my love" (v. 9).

"My command is this: Love each other as I have loved you" (v. 12).

"I have called you friends" (v. 15).

"You did not choose me, but I chose you" (v. 16).

"This is my command: Love each other" (v. 17).

Paul writes to the Christians in Rome, "Be devoted to one another in brotherly love. Honor one another above yourselves" (Rom. 12:10). "Accept one another, then, just as Christ accepted you, in order to bring praise to God" (15:7). Peter tells us to "love one another deeply, from the heart" (1 Peter 1:22). When we choose, love, and accept one another deeply from the heart, we affirm whose we are as brothers and sisters in Christ. By encouraging and building one another up, the body of Christ provides strength and protection in a world where independence and isolation are championed. Where did Satan try to derail Jesus' identity? Alone in the wilderness. Bonhoeffer writes,

Sin demands to have a man by himself. It withdraws him from the community. The more isolated a person is, the more destructive will be the power of sin over him, and the more deeply he becomes involved in it, the more disastrous is his isolation. Sin wants to remain unknown. It shuns the light. In the darkness of the unexpressed it poisons the being of the whole person.[13]

In community, through the power of the Holy Spirit, we practice being the living presence of Jesus to one another. We confess our sins and receive the confessions of others, bearing each other's burdens just as Christ bore our sins on the cross. Remember, you are not called chosen, loved, and accepted to keep it to yourself. Whatever it takes, engage yourself in Christian community.

There is a radical mystery present when followers of Jesus meet together in churches and basements, over coffee and in boardrooms, in living rooms and restaurants. It is in community where we silence all the noise thrown at us throughout the day and affirm our true spiritual identity. In community, our hearts receive the ongoing restoration they so desperately need.

Authentic Restoration

Every Thursday night at our church, a group of men and women meet for a couple of hours to encourage one another in the ways of Jesus and the restoration of their hearts. Aptly named, the group is called "Restoration Thursdays," and in this setting they remind one another of the truth of whose they are in Christ. They do not claim to live lives of spiritual perfection. No, frankly, they come to Restoration because their lives are (or have been) a complete mess—because of addictions to drugs, alcohol, sex, gambling, food, overspending, or any other dysfunction. Meeting together to support one another in a community that favors love over judgment, they drop the bulletproof False Self by acknowledging there is only one true God, and they are not him. The people of Restoration have discovered the beauty of God's design for his beloved bride, the church—a safe place for broken sinners to live out the dangerous message of Jesus and follow in his footsteps.

If there is a group that consistently practices what it means to live in daily surrender to God and practices the ongoing restoration of their hearts, it is Alcoholics Anonymous. Why isn't there an AA group or a similar Restoration recovery ministry in every church across America? This gum-chewing, cookie-eating, coffee-drinking community of cussing smokers contains some of the most authentic, spiritual people I know. These people are some of the rascally, scabby-mouthed sinners whom many Christians don't want in their churches.

And this is the problem with so many churches in America. They want perfect sheep that are comfortable pretending they don't sin anymore. Sin is messy. We feel awkward around someone who is struggling. We are so quick to forget that Jesus came for sinners, not the righteous. Blinded by our own pride, we hide behind our "good" reputations and roles in the church, our false masks and upfront personalities, our strengths and competencies, all in the attempt to hide the sin, shame, and guilt that prefers darkness over light. The irony of it all is that the most basic essentials of the gospel and the Great Commission are being rigorously pursued and applied by the most unlikely people in our culture (i.e., AA), many of whom don't attend church. An alcoholic or addict knows, "If I don't stay on this twelve-step path, I will eventually die. If I am not committed to God first, then my sobriety, everything I touch around me, will also die."

In mentioning the amazing work of Restoration and AA, I am not just talking about alcoholics or drug addicts, I am speaking of everyone who hungers and thirsts for the authentic restoration and daily recovery of their hearts. All of us long for authentic restoration. Is a life like this really possible? How can we follow the ways of Jesus to be and live like loved and accepted children of God?

First, we must understand that true spiritual transformation is a lifelong process. As we follow Jesus, the Holy Spirit is continually forming our identities into the image of Christ. Struggles, setbacks, challenges, heartache, and brokenness are an integral part of this process as God shapes our lives like a potter forms a new creation on a potter's wheel.

Second, a life of spiritual restoration and transformation is marked by a series of biblical processes that define the life of a follower of Jesus. Many of today's churches put far too great an emphasis on "challenging" Christians to do more and serve more than on offering specific spiritual guidance on what it actually means to live as a child of God by being a disciple of Jesus. We are big on challenge, small on spiritual direction.

Spiritual disciplines are the training tools that God provides and uses for us to experience his presence and grace in our lives. The spiritual disciplines are not meant for only superspiritual people, nor are they overtly complicated; they are designed for every child of God who longs to live in the loving presence of God. Living as a child of God involves a growing understanding of and experience in both personal and corporate spiritual discipline. To name a few: prayer, study, solitude, giving, service, confession, fellowship, worship, and celebration.

The Twelve Steps is a wonderful, intentional process that helps us practice many of the spiritual disciplines we must use to live as children of God within the body of Christ. Spend some time reflecting on these twelve steps. Pour over these verses. Ask yourself, "How can I experience greater freedom and joy in my life if I begin to practice these spiritual disciplines with two or three trusted friends?"

Step One is about recognizing our brokenness. We admitted we were powerless over the effects of our separation from God—that our lives had become unmanageable (Romans 7:18).

Step Two is about the birth of faith in us. We came to believe that a power greater than ourselves could restore us to sanity (Philippians 2:13).

Step Three involves a decision to let God be in charge of our lives. We made a decision to turn our will and our lives over to the care of God as we understood him (Romans 12:1).

Step Four involves self-examination. We made a searching and fearless moral inventory of ourselves (Lamentations 3:40).

Step Five is the discipline of confession. We admitted to God, to ourselves, and to another human being the exact nature of our wrongs (James 5:16).

Step Six is an inner transformation called repentance. We were entirely ready to have God remove all these defects of character (James 4:10).

Step Seven involves the transformation or purification of our character. We humbly asked him to remove our shortcomings (1 John 1:9).

Step Eight involves examining our relationships and preparing ourselves to make amends. We made a list of all persons we had harmed and became willing to make amends to them all (Luke 6:31).

Step Nine is about the discipline of making amends. We made direct amends to such people wherever possible, except when to do so would injure them or others (Matthew 5:23–24).

Step Ten is about maintaining progress in recovery. We continued to take personal inventory, and when we were wrong, promptly admitted it (1 Corinthians 10:12).

Step Eleven involves the spiritual disciplines of prayer and meditation. We sought through prayer and meditation to improve our conscious contact with God as we understood him, praying only for knowledge of his will for us and the power to carry that out (Colossians 3:16).

Step Twelve is about ministry. Having had a spiritual awakening as the result of these steps, we tried to carry this message to others and to practice these principles in all our affairs (Galatians 6:1).

Belonging to Christ is all about the restoration of your heart and daily listening to his voice in your life. The spiritual disciplines, practiced alone and in corporate worship, help you hear the tender voice of Christ as a chosen, loved, and accepted child of God.

Next Steps

One morning as I was leaving for a walk in the nearby coastal hills, Aidan asked to come with me. I told my four-year-old that I would love for him to come with Daddy, but he had to go to preschool that morning. "Okay," Aidan said. "Let me just walk to the corner with you." So Aidan strolled to the corner of our block with me.

As I walked and looked down on his little blond head, Aidan skipped along with a big smile on his face, humming a tune like only a four-year-old can do. It was so much fun watching him skip. I felt such joy. Moments like these are one of the many gifts of fatherhood. Little blond hair bouncing around, not a care in the world. Oh, to be four again.

We reached the corner. I gave him a hug and had him run back to our home. Aidan tore off, and when he reached our driveway, he screamed, "Bye, Daddy!"

"Good-bye, Aidan . . . I love you!'

"I love you more," he yelled back.

"No, I love you more than more!"

"No, Daddy, I love you billions more!"

His little round face lit into a big smile. A flash of white teeth, and he dashed inside, happy to get the last word in.

I headed off for my walk. Soon, I was strolling through the familiar dirt path of the fields above the headland cliffs that overlook the Pacific Ocean in North San Clemente. My mind was jumping back and forth as I thought about my upcoming day, but I tried to stay focused on the beauty of the hills and ocean around me.

As I neared the cliffs, a thought suddenly crossed my mind. I said to myself, "I'm not alone here." It was one of those rare times when I sensed God walking with me.

His Holy Spirit was present. He wanted to remind me of something very important.

A picture emerged in my mind's eye. I saw Aidan skipping. The joy I felt twenty minutes earlier resurfaced. I smiled as I thought about how much I love him. How much I love all my children. Tears welled up in my eyes as I asked God, "Lord, do you feel such joy walking with me? Do you take such pleasure watching me walk through these fields as I do when I see Aidan?"

I didn't hear an audible voice. I didn't need to. In my heart I already knew the answer. The answer was a resounding yes! The words of my heavenly Father, completely consistent with everything he has said to me again and again through the truth of his Word, whispered into my heart. *Yes, you do give me great pleasure. You are my son, my beloved, in whom I'm well pleased.*

I reached the cliffs overlooking the Pacific. Standing on the edge, I could see the blunt nose of Dana Point to the north and its surrounding harbor. To the south was Cotton's Point, the home of Richard Nixon's western White House, where my friend John and I surf. Before me was the wide expanse of the deep, powerful ocean. I gazed at the magnificent view. I took a deep breath and soaked up at the majesty of God's creation and thought of Paul's prayer for the Ephesians,

> And I pray that you, being rooted and established in love, may have power, together with all the saints, to grasp how wide and long and high and deep is the love

of Christ, and to know this love that surpasses knowledge—that you may be filled to the measure of all the
fullness of God.

Ephesians 3:17–18

Just how wide, how long, how high, how deep is the
love of God that he would choose, love, and accept me,
not as I wish myself to be but just as I am? Could God
be saying to you and me, through the words of Aidan,
"I love you more, billions more, far more than you can
ever conceive"?

Do you know that you're chosen, loved, and accepted?
I hope you do by now. This is the deepest truth of who
you are. When you know deep inside your heart that you
are chosen and no one can take this away from you, you
are secure. When you know you are intimately loved,
you can live large. When you know you are accepted just
for who you are and that your future is secure for today
and all eternity, you are free. Moment by moment, your
heavenly Father whispers these loving words of freedom
to you: *You are my child, whom I love, my beloved, in whom
I'm well pleased.*

These are words to live by. This truth, this longing to
be chosen, loved, and accepted was placed in the center
of our hearts long before we were ever born. It was put
there by God himself. And every morning when you
and I awake, the longing will still be there. It won't go
away. It doesn't go away. Our hearts are made to long
for Someone far greater than ourselves. "It's in Christ

that we find out who we are and what we are living for"
(Eph. 1:11 Message).

In knowing whose we are, the longing, *our longing*, is
fulfilled.

In knowing whose we are, we can really begin to live.

Epilogue

As I wrote the final words of this book, I looked out my office window. What did I see? Aidan skipping down the sidewalk in a striped turtleneck and green army camo pants. He was just skipping down to Mary and Delaney's house, not a care in the world.

A holy moment.

Aidan knows that he's loved, and that's all that matters.

He doesn't even have to think about it. He just knows.

Lord, teach us how to live as your children.

Teach us to skip. Free in your love.

Reflection and Discussion Questions

Chapter 1

1. Name a time when you were a child when you remember someone choosing, loving, and accepting you just for who you were. Was it your mother or father? An aunt or uncle? A neighbor? A teacher or coach?
2. Describe an event or time when you felt rejection. What was going on in your heart at that time?
3. Reflect on these words God the Father spoke to Jesus: "And a voice from heaven said, 'This is my Son, whom I love; with him I am well pleased.'" Have you stopped to consider whose you are and how these words might profoundly change your life?
4. What voices do you need to silence in your heart today so you can better listen to the voice of God?

Chapter 2

1. For many people, Steven's story is achingly familiar. Good or bad, how were you named as a child? How has that experience influenced you as an adult?
2. Look at the statements on pages 35–36. Which statements resonate with how you think and feel about yourself today?
3. In Matthew 17:5, God speaks of his great pleasure in Jesus. How does it make you feel knowing God takes great pleasure in you? How can God's view of you help change your view of yourself?
4. How does Psalm 145 offer you a completely different view of who God the Father is as compared to someone who hurt you in the past? Sometimes the pain of our past is so deep it radically affects our sense of identity. How can forgiveness free you to develop your identity as a child of God instead of having an identity tied to a hurtful past?

Chapter 3

1. How we view God ultimately reflects how we view ourselves. Have you ever felt like Mary after she broke the glass sparrow (or worse)? When?
2. After reading the truth of God's Word in this chapter, do you know who God says you are?

3. In what ways have you put your identity or worth in things other than who God says you are as his son or daughter?

4. Respond to the words, "You are immensely worth saving."

5. Why does Jesus ask us to receive his kingdom like little children? How can you live as a child of God today?

Chapter 4

1. Do you consider yourself a spiritual orphan or a child of God through Jesus Christ? Why? Why is spiritual adoption an essential truth to understanding who we are in Christ?

2. List a few ways the Bible says that God is for you.

3. Name a time when you were chosen. How did it make you feel? Now name a time when you were rejected. What was that like?

4. God says you are chosen, loved, and accepted. Name a few practical ways to live out this truth in your life.

Chapter 5

1. Have you ever stopped to consider that you have a spiritual enemy who doesn't want to see your deep-

est longings fulfilled in God? Do you ever discount or minimize the enemy's role in your life? How?

2. How are you tempted to control your life by providing for yourself instead of trusting God to provide for you?

3. In regard to your relationships, whose acceptance, approval, or praise do you seek? Why is their approval of you important?

4. God has blessed us with many things to bring pleasure and joy into our lives. How does pleasure-seeking apart from God leave your deepest longings unfulfilled? How do the three Ps distort our true spiritual identity?

Chapter 6

1. Recall a time when you went through a season of personal brokenness. Maybe you're going through that time right now. How do you think God views your brokenness?

2. What do the difficult times in our lives teach us that the good times do not?

3. Why are we tempted to appear bulletproof when we're not? What are we really afraid of?

4. How does Jean-Pierre De Caussade's prayer encourage you to trust God even when you don't understand what he's doing? What is one area in your life that you need to entrust to God today?

Chapter 7

1. Our "what ifs" are fear's best friends. What are some of the what ifs that keep you stuck in your relationship with God and others?
2. There is also a creative side to our what ifs. What changes, possibilities, and dreams can develop by facing your fears?
3. What is true about who you are as a child of God today?
4. How can remembering what is true about who you are help you to overcome the challenges you're facing today?
5. Read Romans 8:15. When you are struggling with fear, who does this verse encourage you to cry out to?

Chapter 8

1. What particular kind of "noise" is most distracting to your relationship with God?
2. Describe what happens when you pursue a relationship with God through prayer. What difference does it make in your life?
3. Where does rest fit in your weekly schedule? What is your life like when you are not well rested?
4. How can intentional times of reflection help you develop a deeper relationship with God and others?

5. What kind of recreation renews you and brings passion back into your life?

Chapter 9

1. What is the single most important message of this book?
2. How can the truth of whose you are continue to transform your life?
3. Perhaps you've felt like a lost sheep that keeps getting locked out of every port (church) you try to enter. What kind of risks are involved with entering Christian community? What benefits can be yours?
4. How do the spiritual disciplines have a place in your life? How can practicing spiritual disciplines help you grow closer to God?
5. Who in your life needs to hear they are chosen, loved, and accepted by God?

Notes

1. Thomas Merton, *No Man Is an Island* (Orlando: Harcourt Brace, 1955), xiii.

2. C. S. Lewis, *Mere Christianity* (San Francisco: Harper SanFrancisco, 2001).

3. Charles de Foucauld, *Fifteen Days of Prayer*, trans. Victoria Hebert et al. (Liguori, MO: Liguori Publications, 1999).

4. Dallas Willard, *Renovation of the Heart* (Colorado Springs: NavPress, 2002), 46.

5. Ibid.

6. Henri Nouwen, *Life of the Beloved* (New York: Crossroad Publishing, 1992).

7. Buddy Owens, *The Way of a Worshipper* (San Clemente, CA: Maranatha! A division of the Corinthian Group, 2002), 68.

8. Philip Yancey, *What's So Amazing about Grace?* (Grand Rapids: Zondervan, 1997), 182.

9. Jean-Pierre De Caussade, *The Sacrament of the Present Moment* (Glasgow: William Collins and Son, 1981), 56.

10. Henri Nouwen, as quoted in a Laity Lodge brochure, Laity Lodge, Kerrville, TX.

11. Dietrich Bonhoeffer, *Life Together* (New York: Harper & Row, 1954), 21.

12. Richard C. Paddock, "A Shipload of Sheep without a Harbor," *Los Angeles Times*, October 12, 2003.

13. Bonhoeffer, *Life Together*, 112.

Joey O'Connor is the author of sixteen books. He serves as a pastor at Coast Hills Community Church in Aliso Viejo, California. He is also the founder and executive director of the Grove Center of the Arts, a ministry dedicated to nurturing the spiritual development and creative vision of artists in the church. Joey, his wife, Krista, and their four children live in San Clemente, California.

You can reach Joey O'Connor at his website www.joeyo.com or by writing to him at:

P.O. Box 3373
San Clemente, CA 92674-3373

For more information about the Grove Center of the Arts, please call (949) 369-6767 or visit their website at www.thegrovecenter.org.

Joey O'Connor's works include:

I Love You Unconditionally . . . On One Condition
I Know You Love Me, but Do You Like Me?
Women Are Always Right & Men Are Never Wrong
You're Grounded for Life & 49 Other Crazy Things Parents Say
Breaking Your Comfort Zones
Children and Grief: Helping Your Child Understand Death
In His Steps: The Promise
So What Does God Have to Do with Who I Am?
So What's the Deal with Love?
So What Difference Does Faith Make in My World?
Excuse Me! I'll Take My Piece of the Planet Now
Whadd'ya Gonna Do? 25 Steps for Getting a Life
Where Is God When . . . 1001 Answers to Questions Students Are Asking
Graffiti: Devotions for Guys by J. David Schmidt with Joey O'Connor
Graffiti: Devotions for Girls by J. David Schmidt with Joey O'Connor

More from Joey O'Connor . . .

Using I Corinthians 13, Joey O'Connor offers fresh insights into
the marvelous, messy, and often mundane moments of married life.